Irene T. Murgan

To Von

Irene T. Murgan

A Taste in Time

Beverley Sutherland Smith's
60 Minute Menus

OMEGA BOOKS

Prawns in Garlic Cream Sauce
Racks of Lamb with Port & Sultana Sauce
Cantaloup with Raspberries & Rosewater Sauce
(see p. 40)

SUMMER

A Taste in Time

This edition published 1984 by Omega Books Ltd,
1 West Street, Ware, Hertfordshire, under licence
from the proprietor.

Copyright © Beverley Sutherland Smith 1981

ISBN 0 907853 08 0

Printed and bound in Hong Kong by South China Printing Co.

CONTENTS

INTRODUCTION

Some years ago, with light-hearted enthusiasm, I began a series of cooking classes entitled 'The Sixty Minute Gourmet' with the idea of teaching busy people how to cook an entire meal in less than an hour. It was co-ordinated so that there was no wasted time in preparation or cooking and it became a study in time and motion in the kitchen. The result was beautiful and interesting meals and it developed into a more serious study into fast cooking.

Meats, for example, had to be cut differently. You can't possibly cook a leg of lamb within an hour, but once boned and flattened, it cooks to perfection in 45 to 50 minutes. Sauces are made by rapid boiling to reduce, or kept very fresh and light. Vegetables and fruits are used in season to make interesting combinations.

The popularity of the classes indicated that there are many busy people who enjoy cooking but have only limited time.

These recipes are not the sort that can be whipped up from tins or packages which have conveniently been kept in the cupboards for unexpected guests. They don't include complicated sauces, glazes, slow-cooked braised dishes or casseroles but rely on fresh food, seasonal fruit, salads and quickly cooked meats and fish.

It is written in the belief that quickly cooked dishes should still have elegance, look beautiful and taste delicious.

There are some things which you may enjoy at dinners but which are missing from these menus. For example I haven't used any soups in the book. No tinned soup ever tastes special enough to me for my family or guests, but home-made soup, requiring stock, takes too much time to fit into this concept of 60 minutes. There are no pastries, crêpes or baked puddings, all of which need to be done in several stages.

There will be sceptics who read the menus and immediately decide that they appear formidable and can't possibly be cooked in the given time. I do agree that it is difficult to give definite statements as to how long a dish takes in the preparation as we all vary in our ability to chop, sauté, and mix. But there isn't a single menu in the book which I can't cook easily within the space of an hour.

There are some factors which are important in using this book. It is necessary to read all the recipes thoroughly before you start to prepare a meal. The suggested order of preparation has been written as a guide-line, covering the major steps, leaving all the smaller jobs to be finished in any order you choose while the meats, etc are cooking. Place all the ingredients out in one area before you start to cook and don't try to cook without good equipment. Sharp knives are essential as is a good, solid chopping board. It is a help if you have a food processor, although all the recipes can be prepared by hand and still take less than an hour.

When shopping, considerable time is saved if you buy foods ready trimmed or cut. For example, buy chicken cut into portions if this is what the recipe states; order meats boned or trimmed in advance from the butcher; buy your fish already filleted and prawns peeled.

Although the preparation and cooking can be done in an hour this doesn't have to be done at the last moment. Many of the dishes can be prepared in advance if you find this easiest, leaving the final cooking for the evening. You can trim vegetables, wrapping them tightly, whip cream, etc.

I find that it helps to have some staples in the kitchen. I always have a big container of breadcrumbs which have been made from stale bread, either frozen or refrigerated. I make up a jar of French dressing ready for mixing with salads. It's a basic oil and vinegar dressing seasoned with salt and pepper. Garlic or herbs don't improve by leaving them in the dressing and these additional seasonings can be added later. Just shake the jar rapidly before using and the dressing will thicken immediately.

I make chicken stock once a month and keep this on hand, frozen in small containers in the freezer or kept for a short time in the refrigerator. Made from chicken livers and giblets with a little added salt, it takes only a short time to cook and when strained, can be used to add flavour to many sauces or meats. Stock cubes can be used but have little flavour and are often too salty when sauces are reduced.

Herbs increase the flavour of many foods and supplies of dill, various parsleys, mint and coriander can be obtained at the market during many months of the year. A small herb garden or pots with cuttings will also supply additional herbs such as basil, thyme, tarragon and rosemary during summer, autumn and spring. Dried herbs can be substituted during winter but should only be regarded as a substitute for the real thing.

You can change these menus around if you wish, after all the main purpose of a book on food is to provide stimulating ideas in the kitchen. They have however been chosen with much thought, not only with regard to the preparation time but also for taste, texture and appearance.

Dinners serve four people unless otherwise stated. But you can quite simply double the given quantities without any problems. In most cases only minutes are added to the cooking time.

So often people believe that beautiful food means endless preparation and cooking time when often the opposite is true. The final result is really what counts and I hope that this book gives busy people more opportunity to enjoy the company of their family and friends by spending less time in the kitchen while not lowering in any way the standards of fine food.

SPRING

MENU

LUNCH   *Serves 4*

Prawns Cipriani

Chocolate Coconut Torte

Suggested Accompaniment
Green salad

Order of Preparation
1. Prepare and cook the chocolate torte.

2. Peel the tomato and dice for the sauce.

3. If not ready to cook the prawns, chop the various ingredients for the dish but keep them separate. They will only need a few minutes' cooking.

4. Prepare the greens for a salad.

Guiseppe Cipriani, who died in 1980 was one of the best-known citizens of Venice. Most tourists to Europe considered it almost obligatory to have a drink at his famous 'Harry's Bar' which was immortalised in Ernest Hemingway's book 'Across the River and into the Trees'. The list of famous people who have sat at the bar would fill a book: Somerset Maugham, Toscanini, Orson Welles, the Aga Khan, Barbara Hutton and an occasional King and Queen.

Across the water from Harry's Bar, set in formal gardens on the island of Guidecca is a hotel also created by Cipriani with an equally famous reputation and guest list. The Cipriani Hotel is luxurious and friendly. Its unique position provides seclusion for its guests yet it is only a few minutes' ferry ride to the Piazza San Marco.

One of the Cipriani Hotel's most famous dishes is Prawns Cipriani. It must be cooked and served at the last moment and would be an ideal dish to prepare at the table in front of guests. As well as making a perfect luncheon dish it can also be served as a first course, although in Venice it is often served as a main dish, frequently following the large platters of pasta which are freshly made each day. All you need with this is salad, some crusty bread for any little bits of sauce which may remain, and a glass of white wine.

The dessert is not Italian at all but a rich, crunchy chocolate torte which can be made and served warm or cold.

PRAWNS CIPRIANI

2 ripe tomatoes	*2 tablespoons oil*
500 g (1 lb) peeled raw prawns (see Note)	*1 tablespoon capers*
flour	*1 tablespoon pickled cucumber, finely chopped*
salt and pepper	*45 g (1½ oz) butter*

Place the tomatoes into a small basin or cup. Pour boiling water over them to cover and leave for 10 seconds, after which the skin should be easy to remove.

Mix some flour with salt and pepper. Dip the prawns lightly in this and shake away any excess, heat the oil and add the prawns. They will take 4 to 5 minutes to cook. As they are cooking, turn them over in the pan.

Meanwhile, chop the capers roughly and mix with the chopped cucumber. Cut the tomatoes into small dice. When the prawns are ready, add the capers, cucumber, butter and tomatoes and stir quickly. The butter will melt and form a sauce with the tomato around the prawns. Cook them for 1 minute longer (don't allow the melted butter to become oily) and serve immediately with a green salad.

Note: If you can only buy prawns in the shell, double the quantity.

CHOCOLATE COCONUT TORTE

This torte is served in the dish in which it is cooked. A pie dish or any shallow round dish can be used, it should be approximately 20 cm (8 in) in diameter. Butter it well so that the torte will slide away easily when cut. Although the mixture can be made by hand, an electric mixer is much quicker.

This recipe makes 6 generous servings but leftover torte keeps perfectly well for several days.

4 egg whites	*3 tablespoons cocoa*
1 cup (8 oz) caster (powdered) sugar	*½ teaspoon almond essence*
1 cup (3 oz) desiccated coconut	

Beat the egg whites until stiff. Add the sugar gradually and beat again for a few minutes until the mixture is shiny.

Mix the desiccated coconut, cocoa and almond essence in a small basin. Fold into the meringue with a spatula. Spread into the buttered dish and place into a moderate oven, 180°C (350°F/Gas 4) for 20 to 25 minutes or until the top is set and it is well cooked on the edges. It is nicest slightly soft and will firm a little as the mixture cools.

Leave at room temperature. It can be served warm or cold, cut into wedges and accompanied by vanilla ice cream or lightly whipped, unsweetened cream.

MENU

SPRING

LUNCH *Serves 4*

Asparagus with Orange-Flavoured Eggs

Strawberries in Port

Suggested Accompaniments
Rolled or folded circles of ham
Salad of various greens

Order of Preparation
1. Place water on to boil for the asparagus.

2. Trim and prepare the asparagus for cooking.

3. Prepare the strawberries and sauce and place into the refrigerator to chill.

4. Beat eggs with orange, ready to cook.

Once I see the first fragile blossoms on the fruit trees and pale green asparagus appearing in the markets, it seems like spring, regardless of the weather. Asparagus may trail into the early part of summer but is really at its best for only a few early months.

Fresh asparagus is one of the loveliest of all first courses and perfect for a luncheon. In England melted butter is still the favourite sauce, and in France Hollandaise sauce is the inevitable accompaniment. There are of course dozens of other variations but take care not to detract from the appearance and flavour by overwhelming the delicate taste. The asparagus in this lunch is served with lightly scrambled eggs flavoured with a little orange. As I mention in the recipe it is important to keep the eggs soft and creamy and barely set. If you overcook them the dish will be spoilt.

I find an asparagus steamer an unnecessary appliance in a kitchen and even though I serve asparagus frequently, I always cook it in water in a frying pan. It is easy to remove with an egg slice and the tips don't disintegrate as they would if it was cooked in a saucepan.

The asparagus can be served on its own with the eggs. Alternatively, add slices of ham to the platter, and follow this with a salad made with lettuce, a little cucumber and shredded celery.

Although you can buy strawberries during the spring months, they lack the flavour of the summer ones. However the addition of the port and sugar in this sauce gives them a delicious perfume and flavour.

ASPARAGUS WITH ORANGE-FLAVOURED EGGS

Fresh asparagus tastes better and cooks quicker if you peel it. 500 g (1 lb) of asparagus with the eggs should be enough for four people, but if the asparagus needs a lot of trimming, buy 750 g (1½ lb).

500 g (1 lb) asparagus	*½ cup (4 fl oz) orange juice*
4 eggs	*salt and pepper*
1 teaspoon grated orange rind	*60 g (2 oz) butter*

Try to buy large fat stalks of asparagus. The thin ones, not necessarily the nicest, are difficult to peel. Bend the asparagus and snap off the tough ends. Using a vegetable peeler or knife, remove the tough thick skin from the stalks. There is no need to tie them in a bundle, just place them so that all the tips are together.

When ready to cook the asparagus, three-quarters fill a large frying pan with water. Season with salt. When boiling, add the asparagus stalks with all the tips facing one way so you can serve them quickly. Boil, uncovered, for 10 to 12 minutes.

If the water boils away, replenish it. Asparagus cooked in this way will remain firm, is easy to remove and unless it is very overcooked, the tips never break off. When ready, remove, using an egg slice and place on heated plates.

The eggs can be mixed while the asparagus is cooking, but must be cooked at the last moment. Mix the eggs, orange rind, orange juice, salt and pepper in a basin. Melt the butter in a frying pan, add the eggs and stir the mixture continuously until it is creamy and just beginning to set. The eggs will continue cooking slightly so take the pan off the heat before they become firm. The secret of this dish is to have the eggs very soft.

Pour a portion of the eggs across the stalks of the asparagus and serve immediately. If you wish you can pour a little melted butter over the asparagus spears. Although asparagus is usually eaten with the fingers, it is easiest in this instance to use a knife and fork.

STRAWBERRIES IN PORT

2 punnets (500 g/ 1 lb) strawberries

¼ cup (2 fl oz) port

2 tablespoons caster (powdered) sugar

Hull the strawberries and place about a quarter of them on a dinner plate. Mash with a fork until pulpy. Place this pulp into a small basin, add the port and sugar and mix with the fork.

Chill the sauce and the berries. Place the strawberries into individual small bowls and spoon some of the sauce over the top. Serve them plain or with sour cream.

MENU

DINNER *Serves 4*

Smoked Fish with Avocado Sauce

Veal Chops with a Cheese Crust

Hot Spiced Cherries

Suggested Accompaniments
Potatoes cooked in cream
(20 mins – p. 95)
or
Garlic-scented tomatoes
(12-15 mins – p. 99)
or
Tossed green salad

Order of Preparation
1. Prepare the fish completely and place in refrigerator to chill.

2. Prepare the veal ready for cooking in the oven.

3. Cook the cherries, which can be reheated as necessary.

In this menu, avocado sauce, pale green and rich in flavour, is served over smoked trout or other smoked fish. The sauce also makes a delicious spread on toast fingers, which can be served as an appetizer with pre-dinner drinks.

It is fifty years since the historic Foyot Restaurant in Paris closed. It is particularly remembered for a veal speciality 'Veal Foyot', which consisted of a large piece of veal, thickly coated with onions, rich melting cheese and crumbs and baked so a crisp coating formed over the meat. A similar result can be achieved by using individual veal chops and coating the top with cheese, onions and crumbs. Not as rich, because it is not cooked for such a long period of time, this dish is prepared and cooked comparatively quickly. Apart from flavouring the top of the veal, the coating also keeps it moist. This is a very popular dish with everyone. I like potatoes in cream as an accompaniment but if you feel it is a little rich, a baked tomato and a salad are lighter.

Hot Spiced Cherries, similar to Cherries Jubilee in flavour, is best made with fresh cherries. However it is now more often prepared with the tinned ones. Usually served with ice cream, it can also be served on its own.

SMOKED FISH WITH AVOCADO SAUCE

Although this sauce is exceptionally good with smoked trout you can use it with other smoked fish too, especially smoked mackerel.

1 avocado, weighing approximately 250 g (8 oz)

2 tablespoons lemon juice

2 tablespoons mayonnaise

salt and pepper

enough cream to give the mixture a coating consistency

1 smoked fish weighing about 250 g (8 oz)

4 lettuce leaves

Cut the avocado in half, twist the halves and they will separate easily, then remove the stone from the centre. Peel them and cut up roughly. Mash the avocado on a plate using a fork. Add the lemon juice, mayonnaise, salt and pepper and a tablespoon or more of cream to make it soft.

Trim any skin or bony pieces from the smoked fish. Place a lettuce leaf on each plate, put a piece of smoked fish on this and then coat generously with the sauce.

The avocado will discolour if kept too long, so you must only place the sauce over the trout at the last moment. But if you wish to make the avocado sauce beforehand, pack into a tiny bowl and cover tightly. It will keep for several hours without discolouring.

Serve the trout and avocado with bread and butter wedges, it is quite a rich dish so do not be over generous.

VEAL CHOPS WITH A CHEESE CRUST

Although only one veal chop is served per person, it should be sufficient as the cheese crust on the top is quite rich. Obviously this also depends on individual appetites, so if you feel this is inadequate, double the topping and use eight veal chops.
Serves 4.

4 veal chops	**Topping**
salt and pepper	1 small onion
45 g (1½ oz) butter	1 tablespoon grated Parmesan cheese
1 cup (8 fl oz) dry white wine	3 tablespoons grated Gruyère cheese
	2 tablespoons breadcrumbs, made from stale bread

Season the chops with a little salt and pepper. Melt the butter in a frying pan and add the chops, cooking them for only a couple of minutes, and turning them once until they have changed colour. Remove them to a shallow ovenproof dish in which they will fit in one layer without overlapping or touching.

Topping
Dice the onion finely and sauté and stir for a couple of minutes in the same pan in which the chops were cooked. Since it was such a brief cooking time, the butter should not have browned. Put the onion in a small basin and add the Parmesan and Gruyère cheeses and the crumbs. There is no need to season this mixture, the cheeses provide sufficient salt. As the onion will be quite moist with butter it should bind the crumbs and cheese together. Press a thick layer of the mixture on top of each veal chop, it is easiest to use your hands to do this.

Pour the white wine around the chops, being careful not to wet the topping. Place in a moderate oven, 180°C (350°F/Gas 4) for about 25 minutes or until the chops are tender and the crust is golden brown. Intended only as a moistening ingredient for the veal, most of the wine will evaporate.

Note: The cheese-coated chops can be prepared in advance, placed in the baking dish, covered and kept for up to 6 hours before adding the wine and baking.

HOT SPICED CHERRIES

¾ cup (6 fl oz) light red wine	3 strips of orange rind, removed with a vegetable peeler
½ cup (4 oz) sugar	500 g (1 lb) dark cherries
¼ cup (2 fl oz) water	1 tablespoon cornflour (cornstarch)
1 cinnamon stick	3 tablespoons brandy

Place the wine, sugar, water, cinnamon stick and orange strips into a saucepan and warm. While the syrup is heating, remove the stalks from the cherries. Add the cherries to the hot syrup and cook, without a lid, for about 7 minutes or until they are tender. Be careful not to overcook them, as if they wrinkle up they don't look or taste as good.

Mix the cornflour with the brandy and stir it into the sauce; it should thicken almost instantly. Remove the cinnamon stick. The orange rind can be left in if preferred as it tastes quite pleasant, provided it did not retain any of the bitter white pith.

It can be served immediately with a side dish of vanilla ice cream or reheated later.

Note: This dish can be made up to 12 hours beforehand and reheated. It is also excellent cold but do not add the cornflour. Cook, add the brandy at the last minute and then when cool, chill.

MENU

DINNER *Serves 4*

Bean Salad with Prawns

Leg of Lamb Maria

Ice Cream with Coffee Sauce

Suggested Accompaniments
Baked potato slices *(30 mins – p. 94)*
or
Potato cubes
with garlic & parsley *(20 mins – p. 95)*
or
Eggplant chips *(5 mins – p. 93)*

Order of Preparation
1. Place the leg of lamb into the oven and prepare the sauce.

2. Place the water on to boil while preparing the beans.

3. Mix up the dressing for the bean salad.

4. Mix the coffee mixture for the dessert.

5. Whip the cream and chill.

With the lighter and new style of cooking in Europe (nouvelle cuisine), almost every restaurant features a salad as a first course, and a high percentage of them are bean salads. They are often combined with seafood, sometimes other vegetables, rare varieties of mushrooms or game. One of the most expensive first courses I ever ate was a green bean and sliced lobster salad, dressed with walnut oil.

The long thin European beans are superb and unfortunately we don't have the same variety here. If you buy very fresh small stringless beans this salad is delicious but if you can only obtain large beans I would serve a different first course. For the best flavour the salad should be eaten within an hour of making it, although the dressing can be prepared and the beans topped and tailed ready for cooking.

The leg of lamb is boned and flattened out so that the cooking time, cut considerably, is close to 45 minutes for slightly pink lamb. If you wanted to serve this menu for larger numbers, it is more successful to buy several small legs of lamb which will cook quickly than to buy a larger leg. The spicy and slightly sweet sauce is delicious with lamb but I have tried it with success over baked fillets of pork too.

I prefer not to serve fruit after this sauce and suggest ice cream with coffee sauce. But you could have a plain chilled fruit dessert, or a chocolate or liqueur-flavoured soufflé omelette.

BEAN SALAD WITH PRAWNS

For the best flavour the salad should be eaten within an hour of making it, although the dressing can be prepared, the beans trimmed and the prawns diced in readiness.

500 g (1 lb) stringless beans	*1 generous teaspoon French mustard*
5 tablespoons walnut oil	*salt and pepper*
1½ tablespoons white or red wine vinegar	*750 g (1½ lb) cooked prawns (shrimps)*
½ teaspoon sugar	

Top and tail the beans. Bring a saucepan of water to the boil, add the beans in handfuls so the water continues boiling and only when all the beans are cooking, season the water with salt. Cook over a high heat, uncovered, for 10 to 12 minutes or until they are just tender. Taste to judge when they are ready. Drain, run cold water over them to cool quickly. They should remain a bright green colour.

Mix together in a bowl, the walnut oil, vinegar, sugar and mustard. Season. Toss the drained beans in this sauce. Do not leave any water on them or it will spoil the dressing. Shell the prawns, dice in chunky pieces and scatter them over the top of the salad.

LEG OF LAMB MARIA

1 boned leg of lamb, weighing
approximately 2 kg (4 lb)
before boning

pepper

1 tablespoon dry English mustard

2 tablespoons brown sugar

30 g (1 oz) butter

1 tablespoon red currant jelly

1 tablespoon lemon juice

pinch cinnamon

salt and pepper

1 tablespoon tomato sauce (ketchup)

The leg of lamb must be completely boned, both the top bone and shank end removed. Where it was boned from the shank end, there will be a high cut. Place the meat on a board so that this is facing you and cut through to make one section of meat which you open out. With a knife, cut into the two thick pieces on either side of the top of the leg to make the meat more of an even thickness.

Season the meat with pepper. Place in a moderately hot oven, directly on the shelf, fat side up and put a tray on the shelf below to catch the drips. Cook this at 190°C (375°F/Gas 5) for 25 minutes.

While the lamb is cooking, mix the mustard, brown sugar, butter, red currant jelly, lemon juice, cinnamon, salt and pepper and tomato sauce together and cook in a small saucepan for 3 or 4 minutes.

When the lamb has cooked for 25 minutes, remove it from the oven. (Also remove the dish which was placed underneath for the dripping fat, as if left in it will smoke in the oven.)

Place the lamb in a baking tray, the meat side upwards, and spoon about half the sauce over the top. Return the lamb to the oven and bake for 10 minutes, remove and pour the remaining half of the sauce over the top. Continue cooking for 10 to 15 minutes or until the lamb is tender. Altogether the lamb should only take 45 to 50 minutes and there will be a lovely sauce around the meat.

Remove the meat to a platter. If you have time it is best to cover with foil and leave it to rest for about 5 to 10 minutes. Cut across in thin slices and serve a little of the sauce on top.

ICE CREAM WITH COFFEE SAUCE

2 tablespoons Espresso instant coffee

4 tablespoons Creme de Cacao

1 tablespoon brandy

½ cup (4 fl oz) thick cream

12 small scoops vanilla ice cream

chocolate coffee beans or a little
grated dark chocolate for garnish

This dessert should be made in small parfait glasses. Alternatively you could use individual dessert bowls.

Mix the coffee and Creme de Cacao with the brandy in a small bowl. Whip the cream until thick. Place a scoop of ice cream in the glass, top with a teaspoon of cream, then a little of the coffee mixture, more ice cream, cream and coffee and top with either the chocolate coffee beans or some grated chocolate. Serve instantly and you can accompany this if you wish with small almond biscuits (cookies).

Note: Instead of Creme de Cacao you can use other liqueurs such as Chocolate Peppermint, Tia Maria, Kahlua, all of which blend well with the coffee flavour.

SPRING

MENU

DINNER *Serves 4*

Salad of Snow peas with Melon & Ham

Baked Squab with Herbs

Lemon Mould with Cherries

Suggested Accompaniments
Baked potato slices *(30 mins – p. 94)*
or
Potato cubes with garlic & parsley
(20 mins – p. 95)

Order of Preparation
1. Prepare the squab ready for baking.

2. Place water on to boil to cook snow peas.

3. Make the lemon mould.

4. Cook the snow peas and finish the salad.

This menu is a rather sophisticated and expensive one, snow peas are a luxury and so is squab, but it makes a delicious dinner for a special occasion. The snow pea salad looks beautiful and is best served on a stark white plate to show the colours and textures.

Pigeons belonged to the local lords under ancient manorial rights in Europe and England and were allowed to roam over the countryside, plundering all the young crops. They were served on the tables of the nobility and the clergy but gradually as the systems of land ownership altered, the pigeons lost their protected status.

A huge enterprise in the United States, pigeons are now bred in Australia, although not in large quantities, and can be obtained both fresh, but more frequently frozen, from the markets.

Devoted parents, the pigeons mate for life, so are expensive to breed. Squab are young pigeons, most of those sold for eating are about four weeks old, any longer and they become airborne and then the flesh is tough and tasteless. The flesh is dark and compact with a rich gamey flavour but it's not too strong for most palates. It can be prepared in many ways, roasted or sautéed, but Baked Squab with Herbs, though very simple is one of my favourite methods of cooking it.

Because of the richness of the flesh you would never serve squab in the same quantities as chicken. Even a medium-sized squab should be cut into two portions. As with many game birds, fingers are better for removing the flesh than knives and forks, apart from removing the breast meat, so finger bowls are necessary.

The tart flavour of the lemon is ideal to finish, very few people ever guess that the dessert is made with yoghurt and the combination assists the digestion of the rich gamey meat. Since yoghurt varies considerably in sharpness, not all the lemon may be needed. If you have clear crystal dishes the appearance is improved by showing the red of the cherries in the base. Old-fashioned saucer shaped champagne glasses are also ideal for presenting this type of dessert.

SALAD OF SNOW PEAS WITH MELON & HAM

These peas are also known as sugar peas and mange-tout peas and while they are usually expensive, the pods have no inner skin and you can eat them all. They are a great delicacy which should be appreciated as a dish on their own.

185 g (6 oz) snow peas	**Dressing**
1 teaspoon oil	6 tablespoons vegetable oil
45 g (1½ oz) pine nuts	2 tablespoons white vinegar
250 g (8 oz) cantaloupe	salt and pepper
185 g (6 oz) ham	2 teaspoons honey

Check through the snow peas and discard any which have large peas, as they will be tough. Top and tail the pods, pulling the string away as you do this. It is quickest and easiest to do this with your fingers rather than cutting the tops with a knife.

Bring a saucepan with some salted water to the boil and add the snow peas. Cook for about 3 minutes only, keeping the water on a rapid boil. Drain them and run cold water over to chill them quickly so they remain a bright vivid green. Drain on kitchen paper and place in a shallow dish.

Heat the oil in a frying pan, add the pine nuts and fry gently for a few minutes until they are golden. Remove them to a small bowl. Peel the cantaloupe and cut into very small dice and mix with the pine nuts. Cut the ham into the same sized dice and mix through.

Dressing

Mix the dressing ingredients well, whisking with a fork and fold just enough into the ham and melon to moisten. Pour the remainder over the snow peas, there will be a lot of liquid but some of it is drained. Leave both the melon and ham and the snow peas in the dressing for about 20 minutes.

Drain the snow peas and arrange them in a fan shape on individual plates, slightly overlapping. Use dinner plates rather than tiny ones, for an effective appearance.

Place a spoonful of the melon and ham at the narrow part of the fan of peas to form a little mound. Moisten with the dressing but don't make the salad too wet.

BAKED SQUAB WITH HERBS

Squab are young pigeons which have not yet become airborne, and are generally about four weeks old. The flesh is rich and gamey but not too strong and they are perfect for fast cooking.

You will have to use your own judgement on how much to serve, according to the size of the birds. Remember that the flesh is rich and you would not serve the same quantity of squab as, for example, a chicken.

2-4 squab	*2 teaspoons freshly chopped thyme*
oil	
salt and pepper	*2 teaspoons freshly chopped rosemary*

Remove the wing tips from the squab and cut each bird in half. Place them on a baking tin, flat cut side down. Brush the top of the birds with a little oil and season with salt and pepper. Mix the two herbs together and scatter it as evenly as you can over each squab.

Place in a moderate oven, 180°C (350°F/Gas 4) and bake for about 25 to 30 minutes. While the birds are cooking, spoon a little of the cooking liquid over the top.

Serve on heated plates, the cut side down. Any juices in the dish can be spooned over each portion.

LEMON MOULD WITH CHERRIES

1 tin approx. 450 g (1 lb) cherries	*2 tablespoons lemon juice*
3 teaspoons gelatine	*1 tablespoon brandy*
2 tablespoons cold water	*1 cup (8 fl oz) yoghurt*
¾ cup (6 oz) caster (powdered) sugar	*½ cup (4 fl oz) thick cream*
grated rind of 1 lemon	

Drain the cherries, the juice is not used in this dish. Divide them evenly between 4 dessert dishes.

Place the gelatine into a cup or small bowl and mix with the cold water. Stand this in a pan of hot water on a medium heat and leave until the gelatine has dissolved. Place the sugar, lemon rind and juice and brandy in a basin. Stir with a fork for a moment to soften the sugar, then pour in the gelatine. Mix in the yoghurt, and whisk using the prongs of a fork. Whip the cream until it holds soft peaks and fold through.

Pour over the cherries. Place the dishes, covered with plastic wrap, into the refrigerator to set. It takes about 30 to 45 minutes.

Note: This mixture can be poured over fresh fruits, such as strawberries, raspberries and sliced Chinese gooseberries (kiwi fruit). It can also be served plain, without any fruit, with a little grated chocolate as a garnish. If you wish to make it in advance, use only 2 teaspoons gelatine.

MENU

DINNER   *Serves 4*

Stir-Fried Asparagus & Onions

Gwenda's Fillet Steak with Caviar Sauce

Glazed Chinese Gooseberries

Suggested Accompaniments
Beans with Kaiser Fleisch
(12-15 mins – p. 89)
or
Tiny new boiled potatoes (15 mins)
or
Green tossed salad

Order of Preparation
1. Place egg on to hard-boil.

2. Trim and prepare the asparagus ready to cook.

3. Prepare the sauce for the steak and trim the meat.

4. Make up the gooseberries and chill the dessert.

The stir-fried asparagus and onions is similar to the Chinese method of stir-fry cooking, where the vegetables remain crisp and full of flavour. It is an ideal way to prepare asparagus and it can be served as a first course or as a main dish for lunch if accompanied by chicken. I feel it is absolutely essential to peel asparagus no matter which way I serve it but especially when preparing it this way, otherwise the dish is full of little hard ends which ruin the taste.

The caviar sauce for the steak is a cold sauce. This may sound strange but it is astonishingly good with meat and if you have any left over try it on some tiny new potatoes which have been boiled in their jackets. Gwenda Bailey who has worked and tested in my kitchen for many years created this one day while trying to find something different to serve with steak.

This is a very light menu, followed as it is by the exotic tasting Chinese gooseberry dish. You could serve the Citrus Soufflé (see p. 25) instead or a hot fruit dessert such as the Apple Cream (see p. 67) if you want something a little more substantial.

STIR-FRIED ASPARAGUS & ONIONS

30 g (1 oz) butter

2 medium-sized white onions

750 g (1½ lb) asparagus

salt and pepper

¾ cup (6 fl oz) chicken stock or water

Melt the butter in a frying pan. Peel the onions, cut in half and place them downwards on a board. Cut in thin half-slices. Cook in the butter for a couple of minutes, stirring.

Bend the asparagus and break it near the tough end. Using a vegetable peeler, trim the outside of the stalks up towards the tip. Although this is time-consuming, it is essential as otherwise the stalks will not cook successfully and can taste quite tough. When trimmed, place them down on a board and cut in long diagonal slices, leaving the tips whole.

Place the asparagus pieces in the frying pan with the onions and cook in the butter for a few minutes. Season. Add the stock or the water and cook over a high heat until most of the liquid has evaporated and the asparagus is just barely tender. This should happen simultaneously, but if the asparagus is still too firm, add a few more spoonfuls of water.

The asparagus can be prepared beforehand and the dish reheated, but undercook it if you do this, so it will not become limp. Serve on small plates; the flavour will be quite superb.

Stir-Fried Asparagus & Onions
Gwenda's Fillet Steak with Caviar Sauce
Glazed Chinese Gooseberries
(see p. 18)

SprinG

Asparagus with Orange-Flavoured Eggs
Strawberries in Port
(see p. 10)

SprinG

GWENDA'S FILLET STEAK WITH CAVIAR SAUCE

4 thick pieces fillet steak

Vegetable oil

Sauce

1 egg, hard-boiled

2 teaspoons lemon juice

1 tablespoon finely chopped parsley

2 tablespoons sour cream

1 teaspoon horse-radish relish

1 tablespoon mayonnaise

salt and pepper

60 g (2 oz) pink caviar

Trim the steak and set it aside. It is cooked at the last moment. The sauce can be made at any time. With this sauce it is most important to add the caviar just before serving, otherwise the colour will change. For this reason black caviar is unsuitable in the dish, as the colour will come out and turn the sauce a most unpleasant grey. The only caviar which does not have this effect is the true caviar, which is now so expensive and rare that if you obtain some, you certainly would not waste it in a sauce.

Sauce
Mash the egg with a fork and add the lemon juice, parsley, cream, horse-radish relish and mayonnaise. Taste and season, but remember that caviar is salty so be cautious with the salt. Lastly fold in the caviar. Heat the oil in a pan and cook the steak over a high heat until it is done to the preferred degree, turning it several times. It should be brown and quite crisp on the outside and either rare or pink inside. Serve immediately with the sauce on the side. The combination of hot steak with the cold sauce is very interesting.

GLAZED CHINESE GOOSEBERRIES

This is a very refreshing dessert but it is important to make it only when Chinese gooseberries (Kiwi fruit) are quite ripe, otherwise the combination of passionfruit with the sauce makes the dessert rather acid.

4 large Chinese gooseberries

3 tablespoons apricot jam (jelly)

2 tablespoons brandy

2 large passionfruit

Place the sauce on to heat while preparing the Chinese gooseberries. Put the apricot jam and brandy in a small saucepan. Warm gently.

Peel the Chinese gooseberries and cut them in slices. Place the slices overlapping on four dessert plates.

If the jam is lumpy, push through a sieve. If smooth and without apricot pieces this is unnecessary. Cut the passionfruit in half and add it to the apricot jam. While this is still warm, spoon it over the fruit on the plates, coating as evenly as possible. Place the plates in the refrigerator and by the end of the meal they will have become sufficiently chilled.

This can be served on its own or with a bowl of lightly sweetened whipped cream.

SPRING

MENU

DINNER *Serves 4*

Stuffed Mushrooms Maui

Racks of Lamb with a Piquant Sauce

Iced Cherries

Suggested Accompaniments
Tossed salad
or
New boiled potatoes with butter
(15-20 mins)
or
Baby squash with rosemary (15 mins
– p. 98)

Order of Preparation
1. Trim the lamb and insert the garlic. Leave them aside ready for baking.

2. Make the sauce for the lamb.

3. Fill the mushrooms.

4. Check over the cherries, removing any bruised ones and chill the fruit in the refrigerator.

The beautiful island of Maui is the second largest in the Hawaiian islands. One section is divided into condominiums and crowded with tourists. The eastern side of the island has been saved from the developers and is partly untouched and quite unspoiled.

In this part of Maui I was served a very spicy mushroom one evening with my pre-dinner drink, filled with egg, bacon and coconut. It was so delicious I obtained the recipe. It was a little too involved to be made within sixty minutes so I have simplified it, but it remains equally delicious.

A little garlic is inserted in the racks of lamb, which are then baked. I buy baby lamb which only needs to be cooked for 25 minutes. It is perfectly trimmed by my butcher so there is little excess fat on the ends. If you have thick, large racks you would need to extend the cooking time by at least 10 minutes.

The piquant sauce with its spicy flavour of mustard and sweet-sour cucumber could be served with grilled lamb chops or cutlets instead if you wish.

The dessert, Iced Cherries, is almost ridiculously simple and yet so good it is worth serving after any meal when something very light and fresh is desired. The recipe brings back memories of dinner parties in Venice. Seated on the outside balcony at the Gritti Palace Hotel, overlooking the Grand Canal, dinner would be served in the open on balmy evenings. The waiters would bring out a huge crystal bowl filled with large shining red cherries resting in iced water and hand you a silver spoon with small slots so the water would drain away. The cold and juicy cherries always tasted utterly perfect.

STUFFED MUSHROOMS MAUI

Stuffing

2 eggs

90 g (3 oz) bacon

1 tablespoon mayonnaise

3 tablespoons finely chopped parsley

1 tablespoon desiccated coconut

1 tablespoon curry powder

Mushrooms

8 large flat mushrooms, weighing about 60 g (2 oz) each

salt and pepper

30 g (1 oz) butter

1 tablespoon oil

Stuffing
Place the eggs in a small saucepan and cover with cold water. Bring to the boil and cook for about 10 minutes until hard. Run cold water over them immediately, so that you can shell them while they are still hot. Mash them with a fork. Cut the bacon into small thin strips and place in a dry frying pan. While the eggs are cooking, sauté the bacon until the fat is transparent and the bacon crisp. Drain on kitchen paper, then place in a bowl and mix in the mayonnaise, parsley, coconut and curry powder. Add the mashed eggs and the fat from the bacon, this will help bind the mixture. Pepper and salt are probably unnecessary but taste to check.

Mushrooms

Remove the stalks from the mushrooms and discard them or use in another recipe as they are not needed in this dish. Warm the butter and oil in a small saucepan. Brush the tops of the mushrooms with this butter and oil mixture. Use the remainder of the mixture to lightly grease a shallow dish or baking tin in which the mushrooms will be cooked. Season the inside of the mushrooms with salt and pepper.

Fill the mushrooms with the stuffing, place in a moderate oven 180°C (350°F/Gas 4) and cook for about 12 to 15 minutes or until they are tender and the filling is heated through.

RACKS OF LAMB WITH A PIQUANT SAUCE

4 racks of lamb, each consisting of
3-4 cutlets

2 cloves garlic

salt and pepper

Sauce

2 tablespoons white vinegar

2 tablespoons water

3 egg yolks

60 g (2 oz) butter

2 tablespoons finely chopped parsley

2 teaspoons French mustard

1 tablespoon finely chopped sweet-
sour cucumber

Slice away some of the skin and fat from the top of the cutlets, but leave a thin layer over the surface of the meat. It is usually not necessary to do this if the lamb is very young. Peel the garlic and cut into thin slivers. Make a cut between each bone on the underneath of the rack and insert a strip of the garlic in the cuts.

Place the meat directly on the rack in the oven with a tray underneath to catch any drips. This way the lamb will cook evenly and not be sitting in fat. Cook in a moderate oven, 180°C (350°F/Gas 4) for about 25 minutes for slightly pink lamb. The meat is seasoned after cooking.

While the lamb is cooking you can make the sauce. Since it can be served at room temperature and will keep successfully for several hours, timing is not critical.

Sauce

This sauce is quickly made but it is essential to use a whisk as the eggs are cooked directly over the heat. A wooden spoon doesn't keep the mixture moving fast enough to prevent it from overcooking.

Place the vinegar and water in a saucepan and cook until it has reduced to about 1 tablespoon. Whisk the egg yolks in a small basin and add the vinegar mixture. Whisk again and then return the mixture to the saucepan; whisk but do not return it to the heat.

Cut the butter into small dice and add half to the eggs. Place back over the heat, cook, whisking until the butter melts and the mixture thickens. If it is getting too hot take the saucepan off the heat and whisk for a moment. When thickened remove from the heat, add the remaining butter and whisk. It should become quite thick and creamy. Place in a small basin, add the parsley, mustard and cucumber and stir through. Taste for seasoning. Cover this sauce to prevent a skin forming; it can also be kept refrigerated and although then very thick, can be placed on top of lamb chops or steaks. It melts down when it comes in contact with hot food and forms a sauce.

Cut the meat down between the bones, placing the cutlets, slightly overlapping on warmed plates. Spread with some of the sauce and serve the remainder separately.

ICED CHERRIES

500 g (1 lb) perfect ripe cherries   1 cup (8 fl oz) water   ice cubes

Leave the cherries on their stalks but check them to remove any fruit which is bruised or broken.

Place the water in a crystal dish and then add enough ice to half fill the dish. Add the cherries and leave to stand for about 20 minutes. The ice will partly melt and cover the cherries and they will become very crisp and cold.

When you serve this it is best to place the dish on a flat plate, so it does not drip as it is served. Guests serve themselves, using either a slotted spoon or a spoon and fork.

MENU
DINNER *Serves 4*

Natural Oysters
with Sour Cream & Caviar

Baked Quail with Bacon & Herbs

Citrus Soufflé

Suggested Accompaniments
Green or mixed salad
or
Sautéed carrots & onions *(15 mins –*
p. 93)
or
Potato cubes with garlic & parsley
(20 mins – p. 95)

Order of Preparation.
1. Prepare the quail ready for baking.

2. Prepare the oyster dish and chill, but don't sprinkle with the caviar until the last minute as black caviar will discolour the oysters.

3. Mix up the base for the citrus soufflé and prepare the dish; the egg whites must be beaten only at the last moment.

Quail are tiny birds, with pretty markings and are one of the quickest of all game to cook. They have many small bones but bred quail have quite a lot of flesh on their breasts. Quail should be cooked quickly and simply and when you serve them have finger bowls of warm, lemony water on the table. Except for removing the meat from the breast, a knife and fork are of little use and it is quite correct to use your fingers when eating these birds.

Although one clove of garlic for each quail may seem a lot, the flavour will be delicate because of the short cooking time and the fact that the garlic is left whole and not peeled. Use fresh herbs for this dish if you can, otherwise use the tiniest pinch of dried herbs, but be cautious as they are stronger in flavour. The combination of herbs and the baking quail imparts a glorious aroma to the entire kitchen. Instead of the herbs I occasionally place a small wedge of orange into the cavity of the bird, skin left on. Wrap them in the bacon and the flesh becomes permeated with a slight but distinct orange tang.

Natural oysters are always popular and our Sydney rock oysters are among the best in the world, rivalling in flavour the much prized and most expensive French oysters, and far superior to the American oysters, the majority of which are coarse to eat. The sour cream base they rest on should be thick enough so that they sit easily back in the shell but don't use too much. Instead of using all black caviar, I occasionally place the black caviar on 6 of the oysters and then top the remainder with pink caviar. The flavour isn't very different but it looks a little more interesting. You can prepare the sauce beforehand, but I think it's best if you complete this dish only about 30 minutes before serving. You must chill it so make sure you have enough refrigerator space for 4 plates.

The citrus soufflé has no complicated base or sauce; it is simply a mixture of egg yolks with lemon and orange rind and beaten egg whites. You can prepare the lemon and orange mixture well before dinner time. Give them another beat for a minute before using however, as they will lose their volume. Use an electric mixer to beat the whites but try not to overbeat them. Overbeaten egg whites will form little lumps throughout the mixture instead of folding through smoothly. I find it best to three-quarter beat them in the mixer, then remove and whisk for a minute to stiffen them completely.

You can't do any of this beforehand but unless you need to finish the meal quickly, it is much nicer to place the soufflé in the oven after the main dish is eaten. It only takes 20 minutes which should just be sufficient time to taste some cheese with the last of the wine or just relax for a moment.

NATURAL OYSTERS WITH SOUR CREAM & CAVIAR

4 dozen oysters	*2 teaspoons lemon juice*
¾ cup (6 fl oz) sour cream	*salt and pepper*
2 teaspoons finely grated white onion	*¼ teaspoon Tabasco sauce*
1 tablespoon tomato sauce	*60 g (2 oz) black caviar*

Remove all the oysters from the shell and set aside. Mix the sour cream with the grated onion, tomato sauce, lemon juice, salt, pepper and Tabasco. Place just a little of this in the base of each shell. Replace an oyster on the cream. Top with black caviar and chill.

The oysters can be served with strips of bread and butter and an additional bowl of lemon wedges.

BAKED QUAIL WITH BACON & HERBS

8 quail	*salt and pepper*
8 sprigs parsley	*8 whole cloves garlic, unpeeled*
8 small sprigs fresh thyme	*45 g (1½ oz) butter*
8 baby sage leaves	*8 slices bacon, rind removed*

Place into the body of each quail a sprig of parsley and thyme, a sage leaf, a little salt and pepper and a whole clove of garlic. There is no need to tie the legs as the bacon will keep the bird firmly in shape.

Melt the butter and brush the outside of the quail, it is easiest to use a pastry brush for this. Wrap one slice of bacon around the quail, making sure you cover the breast. If the bacon is very large you may find it unnecessary to use an entire slice. Secure the bacon with a toothpick and place the quail into a metal baking tin or container. I find they bake more successfully in metal than china.

Roast in a moderate oven, 180°C (350°F/Gas 4) for about 25 minutes turning them once or twice or until the bacon is quite crisp and the quail tender.

CITRUS SOUFFLÉ

It is time-consuming and unnecessary to prepare a paper collar for this or any other soufflé. In many great restaurants, soufflés are served quite naturally mounded slightly above the dish. You will achieve this effect by using a container which holds 5 cups. Butter the dish well and sprinkle with some sugar. Shake out any sugar which does not stick.

4 egg yolks	*1 teaspoon grated orange rind*
½ cup (4 oz) caster (powdered) sugar	*⅓ cup (2½ fl oz) lemon juice*
1 teaspoon grated lemon rind	*5 egg whites*

Beat the egg yolks with the caster sugar until slightly thick, using a hand-beater or whisk. Add the lemon and orange rind and lemon juice. Beat the whites until stiff. Pour the egg yolk mixture into the egg whites and mix gently together.

Pour into the soufflé dish, place in a moderate oven, 180°-190°C (350°-375°F/Gas 4-5) for about 20 minutes or until puffed and golden. The centre should be slightly creamy and still quite soft. This is delicious served with cream or ice cream.

SummeR

MENU
LUNCH   *Serves 4*

**Chicken with Sesame Seeds
& Cashew Nut Sauce**

Baked Pineapple with Rum

**Suggested Accompaniments
Snow peas** *(3 mins – p. 98)*
or
Tossed green salad

Order of Preparation
1. Coat the chicken breasts with crumbs and sesame seeds and chill if not cooking immediately.

2. Toast the cashew nuts and make up the sauce for the chicken.

3. Trim and prepare the pineapple but don't sprinkle with the sugar and cinnamon until you are ready to bake it.

4. Trim the snow peas and cook them at the same time as the chicken.

This is a hot menu, but makes a very light lunch and the flavour and appearance of the chicken dish evokes memories of the Orient.

If the weather is particularly hot you may prefer to serve a chilled fruit dish after the main course. You could slice the pineapple thinly and scatter a little caster sugar over the slices, then a liqueur such as Kirsch. Chill it well until ready to serve the fruit. Another suggestion is to use the Strawberries with Lemon Cream (see p. 29) which has a lovely fresh flavour to follow the sweetness of the sauce over the chicken breast.

SUMMER

CHICKEN BREASTS WITH SESAME SEEDS & CASHEW NUT SAUCE

4 chicken breasts

flour

1 egg, beaten

1 cup (2 oz) breadcrumbs, made from stale bread

½ cup (2 oz) sesame seeds

2 tablespoons + 1 teaspoon vegetable oil

3 tablespoons cashew nuts

3 teaspoons honey

1 tablespoon soy sauce

½ cup (4 fl oz) chicken stock

salt and pepper

1 teaspoon cornflour (cornstarch)

30 g (1 oz) butter

Place the chicken breasts between greaseproof or wax paper and flatten them slightly, using either a rolling pin or the flat side of a meat mallet. First dip them in flour, then in egg. Mix the crumbs and sesame seeds together. It is easiest to do this on a piece of greaseproof paper. Coat the chicken breasts on both sides, pressing the mixture down to make a firm even coating. Refrigerate until you are ready to cook them.

Heat the teaspoon of oil and add the cashew nuts. Fry these gently, shaking the pan to keep them moving, until they are golden. Drain on kitchen paper. Mix the honey, soy sauce, chicken stock, salt and pepper in a bowl. Mix the cornflour with a little water and add. Keep this mixture aside as it is used when the chicken is cooked. Heat the butter and remaining oil together in a frying pan and when the butter is foaming, add the chicken breasts. Turn them once, they will only take a couple of minutes on each side to cook. When ready, drain them on kitchen paper. Discard the butter and oil, there is no need to wash the pan, just wipe it with some paper and return it to the heat. Add the sauce, stir until it comes to the boil and thickens slightly. Mix in the cashew nuts and serve a spoonful of sauce over the top of each chicken breast, distributing the nuts as evenly as you can.

BAKED PINEAPPLE WITH RUM

1 medium-sized pineapple

4 tablespoons brown sugar

1 teaspoon cinnamon

3 tablespoons brown rum

Cut the pineapple in half lengthways, dividing as evenly as possible and cutting through the green top also. Then cut each half into two. Cut along the top of each quarter to remove the tough core which will come away easily in one long strip. Wrap a piece of foil around the green tops so they will not brown when baked in the oven. Place the pineapple quarters, skin-side down, on to a metal baking sheet. Mix the brown sugar and cinnamon together. Spoon a tablespoon of this mixture as evenly as possible over each pineapple quarter. Place in a moderate oven, 180°C (350°F/Gas 4) for 10 to 12 minutes or until the pineapple is just warmed through and the sugar has melted. Do not overcook as the pineapple becomes more acid if overheated. Remove from the oven and peel away the foil. Place the pineapple sections on a serving platter.

Warm the rum in a small saucepan and set it alight. Pour it over the pineapple quarters and take the platter immediately to the table. The sugar on top will make it burn brilliantly. If you prefer, you can pour the rum and light the dessert at the table.

Note: Since this cannot be eaten with a spoon, set the table with knives and forks for dessert. The pineapple wedges are quite easy to cut from the quarters but if you feel this is awkward you can cut them yourself, before the sugar goes on top. (Once cooked it is too hard to handle.) To do this cut the pineapple away from the skin and then using a knife and fork, cut into neat slices. Push them back carefully into place before sprinkling with the sugar.

27

SUMMER

MENU
LUNCH *Serves 4*

**Scallops with Mushrooms
& Pink Peppercorns**

Strawberries with Lemon Cream

**Suggested Accompaniment
Green tossed salad**

Order of Presentation
1. Prepare the scallop dish.

2. Assemble the greens for the salad.

3. Make the lemon cream and refrigerate. Chill the strawberries.

One of the world's first spices, pepper has always been of tremendous importance to civilisation. In cold countries throughout the world where slabs of meat were dried and salted for the winter, pepper provided a spiciness which helped to make it more palatable. The familiar black and white peppercorns were followed some years ago by the hot, spicy green peppercorns and now you can buy pink peppercorns.

They have a light, pickled taste which has an affinity with fish. And they look and taste specially good with the new lighter style of cooking now served in most of the top restaurants throughout the world. Caution is needed however, for while a little is wonderful with the scallops, over-enthusiasm produces a sharpness which will overpower not only the seafood but also any wine you serve with it.

I have suggested a green salad but would serve the scallop dish first and bring the salad to the table later.

The lemon cream is used as a dip for the strawberries rather than being poured over the top. Serve a platter of the berries, it is not necessary to hull them as the top can be used to hold them as they are dipped. Use large ripe berries for this dish, for although the tiny ones often taste as delicious, the presentation is not so effective. Spoon the lemon cream into a bowl and a little of this is placed on the side of each dessert plate so the fruit can be dipped as it is eaten.

Note: You can use other fruits with the lemon cream. Paw Paw (Papaya) cubes are good, cantaloup also teams well and chunky pieces of Chinese gooseberry are delicious.

SCALLOPS WITH MUSHROOMS & PINK PEPPERCORNS

500 g (1 lb) scallops

1 cup (8 fl oz) dry white wine

1 cup (8 fl oz) water

2 slices white onion

375 g (12 oz) button mushrooms

30 g (1 oz) butter

½ cup (4 fl oz) thick cream

1 tablespoon well drained pink peppercorns

salt and pepper to taste

Place the wine, water, salt and onion slices in a saucepan and simmer gently for 5 minutes. Clean the scallops, add them all at once to the liquid and simmer for only 3 minutes. Do not let them boil or they will toughen. Drain, reserving the liquid and discarding the onion slices. Place the scallops on a dinner plate and place another plate on top. This will keep them moist while you finish the dish.

Trim the stalks of the mushrooms level with the caps and if they are not small, cut the mushrooms in half. This dish is nicest if the mushroom pieces are about the same size as the scallops.

Melt the butter in a frying pan, add the mushrooms and cook over a high heat, stirring, for 1 minute only. Pour the reserved scallop liquid over the top and boil rapidly until the pan is dry and the liquid has completely boiled away. Depending on the type of pan used, this takes 4 to 5 minutes. Add the cream to the pan, stir and cook again for a few minutes until this has thickened slightly. The dish can be prepared in advance to this point. Add the scallops to the pan with the peppercorns and reheat. Check the seasoning, you may need a little more salt. Serve in small individual dishes or individual casseroles.

STRAWBERRIES WITH LEMON CREAM

2-3 punnets strawberries, depending on appetites, i.e. between 500-750 g (1-1½ lb)

½ cup (4 fl oz) sour cream

1 teaspoon grated lemon rind

1 tablespoon lemon juice

2 tablespoons icing (confectioners') sugar

It is usually unnecessary to wash the strawberries, but if you prefer, place them gently into a bowl of cold water. Leave for 30 seconds, remove and place on to kitchen paper to drain. Chill them until dinner time. Mix the sour cream, lemon rind and juice with the sugar. Taste, it should be slightly sharp in flavour. Chill the sauce, it will thicken as it becomes cold.

SUMMER

MENU
DINNER   *Serves 6*

**Smoked Fish
with Horse-radish Cream**

Leg of Lamb Trader Vic

Mango Slices in Champagne

**Suggested Accompaniment
Rice with Sultanas & Almonds**
(20 mins – p. 86)

Order of Preparation
1. Place the lamb into the oven and prepare the sauce which is added later.

2. Make the sauce for the smoked fish and chill.

3. Chill the mango but don't cut it until the last moment.

4. Mix the champagne sauce for the mango and refrigerate.

Famous for Polynesian and Oriental food and exotic drinks with extraordinary names, the Trader Vic restaurants are spread across America and now there are several on the Continent and in London. Victor Bergeron, or Trader Vic, as he prefers to be called, is a short man with a craggy face and an expressive, honest but often unprintable vocabulary. Now in his late seventies, he can be found at the San Francisco Trader Vic restaurants most days of the week, where he dines, tastes and creates new ideas.

Chinese ovens, fed by branches of burning bay oak, are used in the restaurants to cook marinated pieces of meat and lamb and these are among the most popular of all their dishes. The meat is marinated, spiced with a mixture of onions, satay spices, lemon and honey. This particular lamb dish was inspired by some of the dishes prepared in Trader Vic's restaurants.

The best accompaniment for the lamb is a lovely aromatic rice dish, tasting slightly of cinnamon and crunchy with almonds. If you have a large platter, serve the sliced meat at one end (with some left unsliced for second helpings) and the pilaf of rice heaped across the other end.

The first course is a fresh and light-tasting fish with horse-radish cream and the dessert makes a perfect finish for this meal: mangoes with champagne.

SMOKED FISH WITH HORSE-RADISH CREAM

This sauce is glorious with smoked salmon, but other cheaper smoked fish such as smoked trout or mackerel are also excellent with it. This recipe is intended as a first course but can also be used as a small appetizer with drinks. Place some of the smoked fish on a piece of lettuce on fresh bread and top with the horse-radish cream and one or two capers.

2 tablespoons mayonnaise

3 teaspoons horse-radish relish or horse-radish cream

2 teaspoons lemon juice

1 tablespoon lightly whipped cream

lettuce leaves

smoked fish, usually 375 g (12 oz) is sufficient but use your own judgement

1 medium-sized onion, finely diced

few capers

Mix the mayonnaise with the horse-radish relish, lemon juice and cream. Taste and adjust with salt, pepper and a little more lemon juice if necessary. Place a piece of lettuce on each platter and top with a portion of the smoked fish, from which you have removed all skin and bones. Coat with the horse-radish cream, scatter the onion on top and then place a couple of capers in the centre. Chill until serving time. This dish can be prepared an hour before serving if you wish.

LEG OF LAMB TRADER VIC

1 boned leg of lamb, weighing approximately 2 kg (4 lb) before boning

salt and pepper

2 onions

2 cloves garlic

2 tablespoons satay spice, powder or paste

¼ cup (2 fl oz) lemon juice

2 tablespoons honey

Have the lamb completely boned by the butcher with both the top bone and shank bone removed. Where it was boned there will be a high cut. Place the meat upwards with this facing you and cut through to make one piece of meat which you open out. The sides will be thick. Cut into these to open it out even flatter and make it more of an even thickness. Place a skewer through the meat to hold it flat while baking. Season with salt and pepper.

Place the lamb in a baking dish and bake in a moderately hot oven, 190°C (375°F/Gas 5) with the fat side up for 10 to 12 minutes.

Prepare the sauce while the meat is cooking. Chop the onions very finely, crush the garlic and mix them together in a small bowl with the satay spice, lemon juice, honey, salt and pepper. Remove the lamb from the dish and drain away any fat, then turn the meat over so the fat side is down, and pour the mixture over the top. Return to the oven, turn the heat down to moderate, 180°C (350°F/Gas 4) and continue cooking, basting several times, for another 35 to 40 minutes. If the sauce starts to caramelise, add a few spoonfuls of water and cover the dish with foil. The meat will still be slightly pink in the centre although when you cut this there will always be a little more well-done meat on the outside of the lamb. The meat can be covered and kept in a warm place for a short time if you are not ready to serve it immediately, and in fact does improve if left to stand for a short time. Remove from the dish, being careful not to let all the onion topping fall away, and cut into thin slices. Spoon some of the onions and sauce over each portion.

MANGO SLICES IN CHAMPAGNE

While fruit served in champagne always sounds exciting, sometimes it can have a very disappointing taste as champagne can bring out a sharpness and acidity in the fruit. I find it more successful if the champagne is slightly sweetened first to make a syrup, then freshened with additional champagne before serving. It's probably not necessary to add that you drink the remainder of the bottle as an accompaniment to the dessert.

1½ tablespoons orange liqueur

2 tablespoons caster (powdered) sugar

¾ cup (6 fl oz) champagne

3 mangoes, weighing about 250 g (8oz) each

additional champagne

Refrigerate the mangoes. Place the orange liqueur, sugar and champagne in a small basin, stir and then chill, covered. With a sharp knife, cut around the skin of each mango to divide in half. Peel the skin from one half, cut the flesh into slices, and put them into saucer-shaped champagne glasses or individual dessert dishes. Half a mango should be sufficient per serving. Turn the mango over, peel the other half and cut into slices. This is an easy way to slice mangoes as by leaving the skin on one side you can grip the fruit.

Divide the chilled liquid between the glasses, top with additional chilled champagne just above the fruit and serve while the champagne is still bubbling.

SUMMER

MENU
DINNER *Serves 4*

Tomatoes with Salmon Topping

Fillet Steaks with Green Peppercorn & Pimento Sauce

Grapes in Honey and Brandy

Suggested Accompaniments
Potato and carrot purée (30 mins – p. 96)
or
Sautéed zucchini (12-15 mins – p. 99)
or
Green salad

Order of Preparation
1. Place the egg on to hard-boil.

2. Prepare the salmon topping and chill.

3. Mix the grapes with the honey and brandy and chill so they will be as cold as possible.

4. Make the sauce for the steak.

In the early seventies two French chefs paid a visit to Australia. It was particularly notable because it was the first time two chefs with world status had travelled so far.

One was Paul Bocuse, black-haired, with a strong patrician nose who created world-wide publicity for the entire Lyons area in France with his Nouvelle Cuisine. The second chef, small and chubby, later became even more famous, as, with his new thin shape he created Cuisine Minceur.

Paul Bocuse and Michael Geurard cooked a dinner for fifty people at 'Glo Glo's', one of the top restaurants in Melbourne. They shopped at the local markets, enthused about the quality of the produce and then created a menu of local fish, duck with pimento and green peppercorn sauce and a soufflé-filled crêpe.

I was fortunate to be allowed to follow them around the markets, watch the dinner being prepared and then eat the final meal. They made the wonderful sauce for the duck during the day, cooking all the ingredients separately. The stock, peppercorns and pimento went into one pan, the wine, brandy, port and cream into another and then they were mixed together. For years I meticulously followed this method, then found that just by throwing everything into the same saucepan, exactly the same result could be achieved. This sauce which is wonderful with steak is also good with duck and reheats most successfully, even days later if you have any over from the dinner.

The tomatoes with salmon topping make a pretty, but light first course and to follow the spiciness of the main course, is a fruit dessert.

Grapes in honey with brandy is refreshing on the palate but other fresh, chilled fruit desserts could be used just as successfully to finish the dinner.

TOMATOES WITH SALMON TOPPING

1 egg	1 small eating apple
4 tomatoes	1 tablespoon mayonnaise
salt and pepper	1 tablespoon thick cream
sugar	**Topping**
220 g (7 oz) canned red salmon	finely chopped chives
2 tablespoons finely diced onion	finely chopped parsley
1 tablespoon finely chopped pickled cucumber	

Place the egg into a saucepan of water and cook for about 10 minutes or until firm. Remove from the heat and immediately run it under cold water to cool it quickly.

Place the tomatoes into a basin and pour boiling water over them, leave to stand for about 10 seconds and remove, the skin should peel away easily. Cut the tomatoes in half and season the cut side with salt, pepper and sugar. If the tomato halves do not sit flat, cut a tiny slice from the base of each. Remove any little pieces of bone from the salmon, then mash the fish. Peel the hard-boiled egg, cut into quarters, place in the bowl with the salmon, and mash with a fork. Add the onion and cucumber and mix through. Peel the apple and grate coarsely, mix this into the salmon and add mayonnaise, cream and salt and pepper to taste. The mixture should be very well seasoned, if too bland add a few drops of white vinegar.

Place a mound of this on top of each tomato half, spread the salmon neatly to the edges and refrigerate. Mix some chopped chives and parsley together in about equal quantities and scatter some of this over the top of the salmon before serving.

Note: Occasionally tomatoes may look ripe and flavoursome but are quite tasteless. If this should happen, after peeling them pour a little French dressing over the top, using 3 tablespoons of oil to 1 tablespoon of vinegar, salt, pepper and sugar.

FILLET STEAKS WITH GREEN PEPPERCORN & PIMENTO SAUCE

Sauce

½ cup (4 fl oz) dry white wine

2 tablespoons brandy

3 tablespoons port

½ cup (4 fl oz) thick cream

1 cup (8 fl oz) chicken stock (or beef stock)

2 tablespoons canned red pimento, cut in strips

2 tablespoons green peppercorns

Beef

4 slices fillet steak

1 tablespoon oil

30 g (1 oz) butter

Place the wine, brandy, port, cream, and stock into a saucepan. (If you don't have any stock, diluted canned beef consommé can be used. I prefer chicken stock because it is lighter. Beef stock can be rather strong when it has reduced.) Cook rapidly over high heat until it has reduced to a mixture which barely coats a spoon. As it stands it tends to thicken a little more. Add the pimento to the sauce. Drain away any liquid from the peppercorns, you can rinse them quickly if you don't want the sauce to be too hot. Crush them, using the back of a knife and add them to the pan. Set the sauce aside and reheat when the steak is ready. It keeps successfully for several days. It may taste strong, but when it is spread on the meat, the heat is lessened.

Trim the steak. Heat the oil and butter in a pan and when very hot add the steaks. Cook them for a few minutes on each side over fairly high heat until the outside is crusty and the meat still rare inside. Salt the meat after it is cooked but naturally don't add pepper as the sauce provides seasoning. Reheat the sauce and spread a little on top of each steak. Serve immediately.

GRAPES IN HONEY SAUCE

1 tablespoon honey

2 tablespoons brandy

1 teaspoon lemon juice

375 g (12 oz) seedless grapes

Place the honey, brandy and lemon into a small saucepan and warm very gently until the honey has melted.

Wash the grapes and remove the stalks. Drain them and place in a bowl. Pour the warmed honey and brandy mixture over them and stir to coat them. Chill. (If they are not really cold when it's time to serve them, place into the freezer for about 5 minutes.)

This dessert can be made 24 hours before using and actually does improve by standing longer in the honey syrup. Serve the grapes in small individual bowls accompanied, if you wish, with a little sour cream.

Note: Honey can vary in strength considerably, I use only 1 tablespoon in this recipe but if you buy a mild commercial honey you may like to use a little more.

MENU

DINNER   *Serves 4*

**Radish or Small Raw Vegetables
with Anchovy Mayonnaise**

Split Chicken with Mustard Coating

**Strawberries with
Banana & Passionfruit Cream**

**Suggested Accompaniments
Beans with sesame seeds** *(12 mins –
p. 88)*
or
Potato Lyonnaise *(25 mins – p. 96)*
or
Onions cooked in white wine
(20 mins – p. 94)

Order of Preparation
1. Place the chicken into the oven to cook.

2. Trim the radishes and chill them.

3. Make the anchovy sauce.

4. Mix the mustard sauce for the chicken.

5. Prepare the dessert and chill.

As a first course, a platter of crudités can be as simple or as spectacular a presentation as you wish to make it. In the first course recipe, anchovy mayonnaise is served with radishes alone, but you could use two or three varieties of vegetables instead. For example, try trimmed baby carrots, small button mushrooms, strips of young zucchini, spring onions, celery, sections of fennel, wedges or strips of cucumber (minus their seeds), or cherry tomatoes. You can buy quail eggs at some of the markets and these look beautiful with their speckled shells. Hard-boil them but serve them in their shell. They are delicious with the anchovy flavoured mayonnaise. Arrange the vegetables and eggs on lettuce or grape leaves.

Scandinavians make a special mustard coating for their Christmas ham which is served as part of the main celebration. The mustard is mixed with egg and it sets into a spicy layer over the meat. I have used a similar idea for chicken. It forms a light, spiced coating over the skin of the entire chicken. Excellent hot, the chicken dish is also good served warm or cold – but not chilled. Instead of the suggested accompaniment of beans, a salad could be served.

The dessert of strawberries with a banana and passionfruit cream is very quickly made. I often use this cream over raspberries or youngberries too. Serve some almond wafer biscuits or small buttery biscuits with the dessert.

RADISHES WITH ANCHOVY MAYONNAISE

This simple mayonnaise is excellent with small crisp radishes but also can be used with other raw vegetables as a first course. When you buy radishes try to obtain the smallest ones. If only larger radishes are available, cut them in half through the centre of the green top.

*1-2 bunches radishes, depending
upon the size of the bunches*

½ cup (4 fl oz) mayonnaise

1 clove garlic, crushed

45 g (1½ oz) flat anchovy fillets

*pepper (no salt is used because of the
anchovies)*

Top and tail the radishes, leaving a tiny end of green on them. Place in water with some ice cubes and leave in the refrigerator to crisp. Before using drain them well.

Mix the mayonnaise with the garlic. Mash the anchovies roughly (do not use the oil from the can) and season with pepper. Add to the mayonnaise.

Arrange a few radishes on each plate with a small bowl for the mayonnaise. They are held by the green tip and dipped into the mayonnaise and eaten with some crusty bread or buttered brown bread strips.

SPLIT CHICKEN WITH MUSTARD COATING

*1 chicken weighing approximately
1.5 kg (3 lb)*

salt and pepper

3 teaspoons vegetable oil

Mustard Topping

1 tablespoon dry English mustard

1 tablespoon French mustard

1 tablespoon Dijon mustard

2 teaspoons sugar

1 egg yolk

breadcrumbs, made from stale bread

Remove the wing tips from the chicken and cut down the backbone using poultry shears or kitchen scissors. Remove the fat from the tail. Place the chicken on a board with the breast towards you and press down firmly with your hands to flatten it. Put it in a baking dish, season the top with salt and pepper and brush with the oil.

   Place in a moderate oven, 180°C (350°F/Gas 4) and bake for about 30 minutes or until the top is slightly golden.

Mustard Topping

Place the mustards, sugar and egg yolk into a small basin and mix together with a fork. When the chicken is partly cooked, remove from the oven and spread the mustard topping over the breast and legs. It will thin down and run because of the warmth. Top with the crumbs, pressing them on gently; it is unavoidable and unimportant if some crumbs go into the dish. Return to the oven and continue cooking for another 15 minutes or until the chicken is tender and the crumbs slightly crisp.

   Cut the chicken down the centre, then cut across the leg and thigh. It will make four large portions.

STRAWBERRIES WITH BANANA
& PASSIONFRUIT CREAM

2 punnets (500 g/1 lb) strawberries

2 bananas

*3 tablespoons caster (powdered)
sugar*

*2 tablespoons orange-flavoured
liqueur*

pulp of 2 passionfruit

½ cup (4 fl oz) thick cream

Hull the strawberries and place them into four individual serving bowls. Mash the bananas on a dinner plate. You should have about ½ cup (4 fl oz) of pulp. Add the sugar to the bananas and mix with a fork until the sugar dissolves slightly. Add the liqueur and the passionfruit pulp.

   Whip the cream until it holds stiff peaks. Gradually whisk in the banana mixture, and then spoon it over the strawberries. Keep one strawberry aside for each dish to garnish. Refrigerate. Before serving, place the additional strawberry on top.

Note: If the strawberries are very tart you can slice them beforehand and add a tablespoon of sugar. Stir and stand for about 10 minutes, so that they will have more flavour under the banana cream.

SummeR

MENU
DINNER   *Serves 4*

Cheese Toasts with Savoury Topping

Veal Scallopini Mediterranean

Apricots filled with Amaretti Cream

Suggested Accompaniments
Eggplant chips *(5 mins – p. 93)*
or
Sautéed potato cubes *(20 mins – p. 97)*
or
Sautéed zucchini *(12-15 mins – p. 99)*

Order of Preparation
1. Prepare the cheese toasts and leave aside for baking.

2. Mix the topping for the cheese ready to cook.

3. Mix the Amaretti Cream for the fruit and chill.

4. Crumb the Veal and make up the tomato sauce.

There is a flavour of the Mediterranean in the main dish of veal, and in the colours and flavours of this entire dinner.

I find the cheese toasts quick to prepare and use them also as a supper dish or a snack. Cut into small squares these could be served as an appetizer to accompany pre-dinner drinks.

Scallopini is one dish which must be prepared with top quality baby veal, unfortunately not always easy to obtain. But good continental veal and pork butchers understand how to buy and cut these meats and although you may pay a little more it is worth it for good veal. Occasionally I add a few stoned black olives to the fresh tomato sauce served over the veal. Mix them in during the last minute to just heat through. They give the sauce a slightly pungent, salty flavour.

To follow these two hot courses, the dessert should be refreshing and chilled. Ripe apricots filled with amaretti cream made with bitter almond macaroons are perfect and ripe yellow peaches can also be used. Serve the fruit on grape leaves or with a few leaves from the garden on the side. An orange dessert or even a bowl of cherries is also good after the veal.

CHEESE TOASTS WITH SAVOURY TOPPING

---

4 slices thick brown or white bread

butter

125-150 g (4-5 oz) Gruyère cheese

Topping

30 g (1 oz) butter

1 clove garlic, crushed

60 g (2 oz) ham, cut in small dice

60 g (2 oz) pimentoes, cut in small dice (see Note)

few drops Tabasco

Toast the bread and remove the crusts. Butter lightly. Cut thin slices from the piece of Gruyère and place these over the top of the toast to completely cover. If you find it easier you could grate the Gruyère but it is a lot faster just to cut it in pieces and the effect is the same when it has melted. Place the toast on a flat tray and into a moderate oven 180°C (350°F/Gas 4) and bake for 5 to 6 minutes or until the cheese has melted. Alternatively you can grill the cheese under a preheated griller (broiler). To make the topping, melt the butter and add the garlic, ham, pimentoes and Tabasco. Cook for a minute or until everything has heated through. Place a lid on the saucepan and set aside, it will keep warm until you are ready to serve the toast. To serve, place the toast on plates and cover with the ham and pimento topping.

Note: Canned pimentoes have a slightly smoked flavour which is distinctive in this dish. You could use diced red or green capsicum (pepper) instead, but it makes a different topping.

Cheese Toasts with Savoury Topping
Veal Scallopini Mediterranean
Apricots filled with Amaretti Cream
(see p. 36)

SUMMER

Chicken Breasts with Sesame Seeds & Cashew Nut Sauce
Baked Pineapple with Rum
(see p. 26)

SUMMER

VEAL SCALLOPINI MEDITERRANEAN

One of the quickest of all veal dishes to cook, veal scallopini will toughen if overcooked. The light, fresh tomato sauce which is served with the veal is also excellent with grilled lamb chops. Instead of scallopini you can prepare the dish using veal chops.

Sauce

250 g (8 oz) ripe tomatoes

45 g (1½ oz) butter

pepper (salt is unnecessary because of the anchovies)

1 teaspoon sugar

2 teaspoons fresh basil, finely chopped or
½ teaspoon dried basil leaves

1 tablespoon finely chopped parsley

30 g (1 oz) flat anchovy fillets, roughly chopped

1 tablespoon capers, roughly chopped

Veal

4 veal scallopini

flour

salt and pepper

3 tablespoons oil

Sauce

Pour boiling water over the tomatoes, and after leaving to stand for about 10 seconds, remove and the skin should come away easily. Chop the tomatoes into small dice. Melt the butter in a frying pan or saucepan and add the tomatoes, sugar and pepper. Cook over a high heat for a couple of minutes, then add the basil, parsley, anchovy fillets and capers. Cook again for a few minutes or until the tomato has just softened. The sauce should have a fresh, light taste. Set it aside and warm again when serving.

Veal

Place the veal scallopini, one at a time, between wax paper and pound them with a mallet until they are of an even thinness. Sometimes the butcher will do this for you which can save considerable time. Season the flour with salt and pepper and coat the veal with it. Heat the oil. There should be a generous film of oil on the base of the frying pan so you may need more than the specified quantity. Scallopini should not be crowded, so either cook them in two batches or use two pans. Cook over a fairly high heat for 3 to 4 minutes or until they are crisp on the outside and tender within. Warm the sauce again, drain the veal on kitchen paper, place on plates and spoon a little of the sauce on top of each scallopini.

APRICOTS FILLED WITH AMARETTI CREAM

Amaretti are little macaroons made from bitter almonds. You can buy these in most shops which sell imported biscuits. You can also use macaroons made from sweet almonds, but you won't need as much sugar. Although I prefer this served with fresh, ripe apricots, canned apricots can be used. It is also very good with strawberries or other berry fruits.

6-12 apricots

angelica

Amaretti Cream

½ cup (4 fl oz) thick cream

1 tablespoon icing (confectioners') sugar

1 tablespoon Marsala wine

3 tablespoons biscuit crumbs, made from crushed Amaretti biscuits

2 teaspoons brandy

To make the Amaretti cream whip the cream until stiff and mix in the sugar, Marsala, crumbs and brandy. Chill. The number of apricots you use depends greatly on the size of the fruit. If they are tiny ones use 2 per person, if large, 1 may be sufficient. Cut the apricots in half and remove the stones. Fill the centres with the Amaretti cream. Cut the angelica into small strips and place a strip on top of each apricot half. Keep them chilled until serving time. You can serve these on individual plates or on one large platter.

MENU

SUMMER DINNER *Serves 4*

Prawns in Garlic Cream Sauce

Racks of Lamb
with Port & Sultana Sauce

Cantaloup with Raspberries
& Rosewater Sauce

Suggested Accompaniments
Baked potato slices (30 mins – p. 94)
or
Potato & carrot purée (30 mins –
p. 96)
or
Baby squash with butter (15 mins –
p. 98) Delete the seasoning of
rosemary if using to accompany
the lamb.

Order of Preparation
1. Prepare the lamb dish ready for baking.

2. Prepare the ingredients for the sauce for the prawns, but don't cook them until the last moment.

3. Prepare the cantaloup and raspberries and chill them until dinner time.

Garlic Prawns, along with Seafood Cocktail and Avocado are always among the top ten of favourite restaurant dishes. It may not seem very imaginative but many people would rather dine out on old favourites than gamble with unfamiliar combinations.

This recipe for garlic prawns is a little different from the usual with the addition of cream to make a light sauce around the prawns. I personally keep the garlic flavour a bit light. Although I have suggested two cloves of garlic, if they are large, one may be sufficient. A prawn dish which absolutely reeks of garlic can be overwhelmingly rich. The same dish is also ideal for lunch, served with a salad and some crusty bread but you may need to allow a few extra prawns if this is all you are serving.

The sweetness of lamb is emphasised in the main course recipe by the sauce of port and sultanas. There is a little garlic in this too, but the cloves are left whole in the sauce and removed before serving. It is such a whisper of garlic flavour I wouldn't cut it out unless you are not keen on garlic at all. I often make the same dish using a leg of lamb; it couldn't be done within sixty minutes, but is worth trying when time is not so important. Roast the lamb first for about 30 minutes to remove much of the fat, discard this and then continue cooking it in a casserole surrounded by the port sauce.

After the robust flavour of garlic prawns and then the lamb, fruit is the obvious choice for dessert. The cantaloup combined with raspberries is refreshing and light. A strawberry dessert would be equally good as an alternative.

PRAWNS IN GARLIC CREAM SAUCE

---

375 g (12 oz) peeled, raw prawns
(see Note)

45 g (1½ oz) butter

2 cloves garlic, crushed

salt and pepper

½ cup (4 fl oz) thick cream

2 tablespoons finely chopped parsley

Melt the butter in a frying pan. Add the prawns, cook for a minute over medium heat, turning them. Add the garlic and season with salt and pepper.

When the prawns have changed colour and are almost cooked, add the cream and turn the heat up to high. Cook until a creamy sauce forms around the prawns. Add the parsley and serve immediately.

Note: If you buy prawns in their shell, double the quantity.

RACKS OF LAMB WITH PORT & SULTANA SAUCE

2 racks of lamb,
each consisting of about 6 chops

salt and pepper

1 cup (8 fl oz) port

½ cup (4 fl oz) chicken stock

1 bay leaf

3 tablespoons sultanas

2 whole cloves garlic

2 teaspoons cornflour (cornstarch)

Trim away some of the excess fat from the top of the lamb, leaving only a thin layer. Heat a heavy-based frying pan. Place the lamb fat-side down in the pan over high heat and cook until the outside of the fat is brown. Neither moisture nor fat is needed in the pan as sufficient will come from the meat as it begins to brown. Cook the racks separately as it is difficult to fit more than one rack in the average-sized frying pan. Remove and season the lamb.

Discard all the fat from the pan, there is no need to wash it but wipe it out. Mix the port, stock, bay leaf, sultanas and garlic together. Depending on the saltiness of the stock, season the mixture with salt and pepper. Pour this into the pan and bring to the boil.

Place the racks of lamb in a casserole (a lid is not required). Pour the sauce over the top of the lamb and place in a moderate oven, 180°C (350°F/Gas 4) and cook for about 25 minutes or until the meat is done to the right degree. Mix the cornflour with some water, add the liquid from the lamb and cook in a saucepan for a moment until it has thickened. This does not take long as the liquid is already hot. Cut the lamb into chops, spooning a little of the sauce and sultanas on each serving.

CANTALOUP WITH RASPBERRIES & ROSEWATER SAUCE

The perfume of rosewater and raspberries has a wonderful affinity with cantaloup. Rosewater can be bought at shops which stock Oriental foods and many supermarkets have supplies. The orange flower water can also be found in many speciality stores or health food shops.

2 baby cantaloups (see Note)

1 punnet (250 g/8 oz) raspberries

2 tablespoons caster (powdered) sugar

1 teaspoon orange flower water

2 teaspoons rosewater essence

1 tablespoon brandy

Cut the cantaloups in half and remove the seeds. Chill while preparing the sauce. Place the raspberries in a bowl. Add the caster sugar, orange flower water, rosewater, and brandy. Stir gently and leave aside at room temperature for about 10 minutes, then chill. Quite a bit of sauce will form around the raspberries.

Place the cantaloups on a leaf on a flat plate and fill the centre with raspberries and some of the juice. Do not serve cream or ice cream with this as it is nicest served on its own.

Note: Although this is nicest if made with baby cantaloups, sometimes they are unavailable. It is possible to use a large cantaloup as a substitute, but the dish is then presented differently. Peel the cantaloup, cut in half and remove the seeds. Cut into thin slices and arrange these on individual plates. Spoon the sauce over the top of the slices.

SUMMER

MENU
DINNER *Serves 4*

Eggs in Vinaigrette Sauce with Caviar

Split Chickens with Toasted Sesame Seeds

Peaches Madame Point

Suggested Accompaniments
Bean shoots with ginger *(5-6 mins – p. 88)*
or
Baby squash with butter & rosemary *(15 mins – p. 98)*
or
Baked potato slices *(30 mins – p. 94)*

Order of Preparation
1. Split the chickens and place into the oven.

2. Put the eggs on to cook.

3. Make the sauce ready for the final stages of the chicken.

4. Mix up the vinaigrette for the eggs and complete the dish if the eggs are cool.

5. Place the peaches into the refrigerator to chill and mix up the strawberry sauce, refrigerating it in a basin so it will be cold by the time dinner is ready.

This is one of the nicest meals of all for a hot evening because, not only is the food beautiful in appearance, but all the dishes have interesting flavours which will appeal to even jaded appetites.
   The egg dish is quite simple: sliced hard-boiled eggs in a Vinaigrette Sauce which has a little sour cream added and garnished with stripes of black and red caviar for a spectacular effect.
   By splitting the chicken down the centre and baking it flat in the oven, the cooking time is cut by about one-third yet it remains just as moist as a chicken roasted in the more conventional way. For easy serving, two small chickens can be cut in half; if only large chickens are available cut it into four. (Two thighs and two breasts.) I have suggested serving vegetables with this rather than a salad as another vinaigrette in the menu would be too repetitive.
   The dessert, 'Peaches Madame Point' was created at the restaurant 'La Pyramide'. At the height of his glory, the late Fernand Point was acknowledged as the greatest chef in the whole of France, gradually changing 'La Pyramide' from a pleasant little inn to one of the most important restaurants in Europe. He created many dishes but cared little for the fame he achieved. After his death his widow continued running the restaurant and despite the sceptics who believed that standards would drop, she has maintained a three star rating.

EGGS IN VINAIGRETTE SAUCE WITH CAVIAR

6 large eggs

1 small jar black caviar
(45 g (1½ oz) size)

1 small jar red caviar
(45 g (1½ oz) size)

several sprigs of parsley

Vinaigrette Sauce

4 tablespoons peanut oil

2 tablespoons white wine vinegar

½ medium-sized onion, very finely diced

1 teaspoon French mustard

salt and pepper

1 tablespoon sour cream

Place the eggs in a small saucepan and cover with cold water. Bring to the boil, simmer gently for 10 minutes. Remove, run cold water over the eggs and leave to cool for 5 minutes. To crack the shells tap them lightly and then return them to the water. This makes them much easier to peel.

Vinaigrette Sauce

Place the oil, vinegar, onion and mustard in a small basin. Whisk quickly with a fork until it thickens. Season with salt and pepper. Add the sour cream and set aside. Simply stir again before using if it separates at all. Peel the eggs and slice them. Arrange on an oval platter with the slices slightly overlapping. Stir the sauce and pour over the top. Scatter the black caviar in a thick stripe along one side of the platter, then scatter the red caviar in a stripe on the other side. Place a couple of sprigs of parsley in the centre if you wish. Accompany with some crusty bread or bread and butter wedges.

SPLIT CHICKENS WITH TOASTED SESAME SEEDS

If you cannot buy small chickens, use a larger one and add 15 minutes to the cooking time.

2 small chickens, each weighing about 1.25 kg (2¼ lb)

2 tablespoons vegetable oil

2 tablespoons lemon juice

1 clove garlic, crushed

salt and pepper

2 tablespoons honey

toasted sesame seeds (available in packets in most health food shops)

Place the chicken on a board so that the backbone is facing you. Using poultry shears, cut alongside the backbone. Do not attempt to cut through it. Remove the fat from the tail of the chicken and turn the bird over with the breast side up. Press down firmly with your hands to flatten it or quickly bang it flat with a rolling pin. Do the same with the second chicken.

Brush a shallow baking dish with half the oil. Place the chickens side by side in the dish with the breast sides upward. Mix the remaining oil with the lemon juice and garlic and brush this over the chickens. Sprinkle with salt and pepper. Place in a preheated oven, 190°C (375°F/Gas 5) and bake for about 30 minutes. Chickens flattened this way cook very quickly. Trickle the honey over the top of the chickens and scatter on enough sesame seeds to form a light coating. The seeds will stick easily to the honey. Bake for a further 5 minutes until the top is golden and glazed. Remove and cover the dish lightly with foil if you are not serving immediately. The dish can be kept warm for about 15 minutes without spoiling.

Cut each chicken directly through the centre and serve half a chicken to each person. If using one large chicken, cut into quarters.

PEACHES IN THE STYLE OF MADAME POINT

1 punnet (250 g/8 oz) strawberries

3 tablespoons icing (confectioners') sugar

2 tablespoons Kirsch

3 tablespoons whipped cream

2 large or 4 small ripe peaches

Hull the berries and either mash them well or push them through a sieve. Do not use a metal sieve as this may darken the fruit. A food processor can also be used to purée. Place in a bowl and mix in the sugar and Kirsch and then add the cream, which should only be lightly whipped so it folds through evenly. Chill the mixture. Chill the peaches in the refrigerator and then when ready to serve, spoon some of the strawberry mixture into either saucer-shaped champagne glasses or individual dishes. Peel the peaches and cut into neat dice or place the peaches on top of the strawberries and serve immediately.

AUTUMN

MENU
LUNCH *Serves 4*

Avocado & Curried Mushroom Quiche Without a Crust

Oranges in Rosewater Sauce

Suggested Accompaniment Green salad

Order of Preparation
1. Remove the peel from one orange and cook.

2. Make the avocado quiche, if not ready to bake immediately you can leave it in the quiche dish for about 20 minutes without the avocado darkening.

3. While the quiche is cooking, finish making the orange dessert.

You probably couldn't correctly call this dish a quiche, as it doesn't have a pastry casing. But served in a quiche dish, it looks exactly like one and is firm enough to serve cut into small wedges. (It is best to serve several thin wedges to each person; you may have trouble keeping large wedges on the serving spatula.) It is a really interesting dish, the avocado flavour intensified by the curried mushrooms underneath. You should be able to taste the curry but it shouldn't be burning hot, and as curry powders vary considerably in strength, adjust the quantity according to the brand you use. It is a perfect lunch dish and can also be used as a first course for dinner. It is quite rich and will serve 6 to 8 people as a first course. Although avocado usually browns quickly, when cooked in this way, it can be kept for up to 8 hours without discolouring. The quiche is excellent warm or cold.

The orange dessert contains rosewater essence which has a perfume and taste of full-blown roses. Use only a little of this as a flavouring, too much is overpowering. You can buy it at some health food shops, gourmet shops, supermarkets or shops selling Oriental goods.

AVOCADO & CURRIED MUSHROOM QUICHE
WITHOUT A CRUST

This quiche is served directly from the dish in which it is cooked. A china quiche dish is nicest for serving. In its absence, use a pie dish or shallow round ovenproof dish. The dish should be 20 cm (8 in) to 23 cm (9 in) in diameter.

This is one of the most interesting recipes I know, with its rich but almost bland avocado flavour intensified in some way by the curried mushrooms underneath.

185 g (6 oz) mushrooms	*3 eggs*
45 g (1½ oz) butter	*¾ cup (6 fl oz) thick cream*
2 teaspoons curry powder	*¼ teaspoon salt*
salt	*white pepper*
1 avocado, weighing approximately 250 g (8 oz)	*3 tablespoons dry white wine*
	1 tablespoon tomato sauce (ketchup)
3 tablespoons finely chopped spring onions (scallions)	

Cut the stalks level with the caps of the mushrooms and slice the mushrooms thickly. Melt the butter in a frying pan and cook the mushrooms over a high heat, stirring until just softened. They should take only a minute. Add the curry powder and fry again for a few seconds, seasoning with a pinch of salt. Butter the dish for the quiche and add the mushrooms, spreading them evenly over the base. Cut the avocado in half, twist,and it will come away from the stone. With the point of a knife, remove the stone. Peel the avocado and cut into slices. Arrange these over the mushrooms and then scatter the spring onions over the top. Beat the eggs, cream, salt and pepper with the wine and tomato sauce in a basin and pour the mixture over the top of the avocado. Place in a moderate oven, 180°C (350°F/Gas 4) for approximately 25 minutes or until it has just lightly set in the middle. When ready, remove from the oven and leave to settle for 5 minutes before cutting into wedges. This quiche is excellent served cold. But it must be eaten the day it is made.

ORANGES IN ROSEWATER SAUCE

4 oranges	*1 teaspoon orange flower water*
¾ cup (6 fl oz) fresh orange juice	*1 teaspoon rosewater essence*
2 tablespoons sugar	

Use either a vegetable peeler or zester to remove wafer thin strips of peel from 1 orange. If you remove them with the vegetable peeler, cut the pieces into thin strips. Place them into a small saucepan, cover generously with water and cook the peel until it is tender. Drain.

Place the orange juice and sugar into the same saucepan, return the peel to the pan and cook over high heat until the peel is transparent and the syrup thick and glazed.

While this is cooking, peel the remaining oranges, being careful to completely remove the bitter white membrane. Cut each orange into half and then into very thin slices, flicking out any pips with the point of the knife. Place the oranges into a serving bowl.

Remove the syrup from the heat and add the orange flower water and rosewater essence. Pour this over the oranges in the bowl. This is nicest served very cold. If you're running short of time, place it in the freezer for 10 minutes before serving.

AUTUMN

MENU
LUNCH   *Serves 4*

Spiced Chicken Wings

Rice with Peas & Bacon

Paw Paw with Passionfruit Sauce

Suggested Accompaniment
Mixed green salad

Order of Preparation
1. Prepare the chicken wings and place into the oven to cook.

2. Slice the paw paw into sections and mix with the sauce, leave to chill so it will be as cold as possible.

3. Prepare rice.

Talking with famous chefs and restaurateurs, it is interesting how many of them admit that their favourite dishes are very simple ones, in complete contrast to the more elaborate creations served to their customers.

Into this category comes chicken wings, rarely served at dinners, yet the flesh on the wing is the sweetest and most flavoursome part of the bird. There are many sauces you can use with chicken wings; these spiced chicken wings have an Oriental flavour and when cooked, are glazed and shiny and rather sticky on the outside. If the occasion is informal and fingers are used to remove the meat close to the bones, provide plenty of finger bowls.

I like rice with them and the rice dish with peas and bacon is quite simple and delicious but if you don't have time for this, serve boiled rice, cooked with a few slices of lemon in the saucepan.

If paw paw is not available to make the dessert, try cantaloup or honeydew melon instead.

SPICED CHICKEN WINGS

When you buy the chicken wings try to obtain the entire wing. Many shops sell only the last section. The part with the most meat, the portion nearest to the breast, is often kept and sold with the breast to make dishes such as Chicken Kiev.

1 kg (2 lb) chicken wings

2 tablespoons vegetable oil

2 tablespoons soy sauce

2 tablespoons tomato sauce (ketchup)

¼ cup (2 fl oz) honey

1 small clove garlic, crushed

¼ teaspoon Five Spice Powder

¼ teaspoon salt

Cut away the tiny wing tips on all the chicken wings. Mix all the remaining ingredients together in a large basin. Add the chicken wings and stir to coat them with the sauce.

Use a flat shallow dish to bake the wings. You can even cook them in something like a Swiss (jelly) roll tin, as they will cook much quicker if in one layer only. They cook faster in metal than in china.

Put the chicken wings into the baking dish with all the sauce. Cook in a moderate oven, 180°C (350°F/Gas 4) for about 45 minutes. Turn them a couple of times during the cooking and check they do not become too brown. If so, reduce the oven temperature. When the chicken is ready to be served, the outside should be sticky and caramelised from the sauce.

RICE WITH PEAS & BACON

You can use either fresh, dried or frozen peas in this dish. All are successful and regardless of which type, are added at exactly the same time. The quantity is not very important, you can have a few studded throughout the rice, or many. I generally use a small handful, about 125 g (4 oz) fresh unshelled peas.

2 tablespoons oil	*3 cups (24 fl oz) chicken stock or water*
1 onion, roughly diced	
125 g (4 oz) bacon, cut in thin strips	*peas*
1½ cups (8 oz) long grain rice	*salt and pepper to taste*
	30 g (1 oz) butter

Place the oil in a saucepan with a tight-fitting lid. Add the onion and fry for a moment, stirring, then add the bacon and cook them both until the bacon fat is transparent and the onion has softened. You do not need to stir continually but just move them around occasionally.

Add the rice to the pan, turn the heat up and stir until it has become slightly opaque and some of the grains are golden. Add the stock or water and peas. Season. It should start to bubble and boil almost instantly. When it is boiling hard, turn the heat down low, place the lid on the pan and leave to steam away for about 15 minutes or until the rice grains are quite separate and all the liquid has been absorbed. It depends on the rice however, so check by tasting and if the pan is dry you can add a few more spoonfuls of liquid. Taste again for seasoning, add the butter and fluff up the rice with two forks, the butter will melt through in the process.

PAW PAW WITH PASSIONFRUIT SAUCE

750 g (1½ lb) paw paw (papaya)	*3 tablespoons caster (powdered) sugar*
2 tablespoons lemon juice	
	2 large passionfruit

Remove the seeds from the paw paw. Peel away all the skin carefully, as any little pieces of skin left on will give a bitter taste. Cut the paw paw into bite-sized pieces and place in a serving bowl.

Mix the lemon juice, sugar and the pulp from the passionfruit together in a small basin. Pour this sauce over the paw paw and stir with a spoon, turning it over until each piece is coated with the mixture. Chill immediately so that by the time it is served it will be cold.

This refreshing dessert keeps for several days if you have any left over. Paw Paw with Passionfruit Sauce is nicest served on its own; cream detracts from the flavour.

AutumN

MENU
DINNER *Serves 4*

Tagliatelle with Three Cheeses

Prawns with Almond Garlic Butter

Platter of Figs & Grapes,
Walnuts & Chocolate

Spiked Coffee

Suggested Accompaniment
Tossed green salad, sliced tomato
& chopped fresh basil

Order of Preparation
1. **Place a large pot of water on to boil for the pasta.**

2. **Prepare the Almond Garlic Butter and fill the prawns. It is not necessary to refrigerate them if they are cooked within 30 minutes.**

3. **Prepare the cheeses ready for the pasta.**

4. **Set out the fruit platter, refrigerate it and have ingredients on hand for the Spiked Coffee.**

On one of my first visits to Rome I had lunch with friends at a small but quite famous restaurant, recognised for its antipasto and home-made pasta dishes. We all ordered tagliatelle with cheese and the waiter appeared with a huge oval white platter, resembling a meat plate in size and three small dinner plates. Expertly he served the tagliatelle onto the three smaller plates and then ceremoniously deposited the huge platter in front of me, explaining that the best flavour of all would be on the large platter. Sticky with cheese and with extra portions of sauce left underneath the tagliatelle, it was undoubtedly the best of the four portions.

You may not want to follow the restaurant custom of serving your tagliatelle this way but their attitude towards the composition of the dish is worth noting. The pasta should be the best quality you can buy, and the cheese should be grated on the day it is to be eaten. Packaged and pre-grated cheeses won't have the same flavour at all. In this sauce there is a combination of three cheeses: Gruyère or a melting type of cheese, Parmesan and a blue cheese, all of which form a creamy mixture around the pasta. For the blue cheese use a Roquefort or Danish blue but be cautious in the amount you add as the blue cheese should not dominate but just contribute a light flavour.

The flavour of the prawns is perfect after pasta; prepared in this way, they are meltingly tender and flavoured lightly with garlic. The almonds are not only used as a flavouring but help bind the butter so the mixture coats the prawns instead of melting away when they are cooked. You can use the same mixture to top oysters in the shell or clams.

The lettuce and tomato salad should be made with a little fresh basil but if it is too late in the season don't substitute the dried herb. Try instead some chopped chives or the finely chopped green top of a spring onion over the lettuce.

The fruit and nut platter is put together with chilled fresh figs and if these can't be obtained, dried eating figs can be used instead. Walnuts in the shell, grapes and chocolate are placed on the table to eat with the coffee. As chocolate can be indigestible after seafood, serve a light chocolate rather than rich, heavy dark chocolate (the fine creamy Swiss wafers of chocolate are perfect for this).

TAGLIATELLE WITH THREE CHEESES

375 g (12 oz) tagliatelle

1 cup (4 oz) grated Gruyère cheese

3 tablespoons grated Parmesan cheese

a small piece (about a tablespoon) blue cheese

1 cup (8 fl oz) thick cream

salt and pepper

Bring a large pot of water to the boil then add salt to season and a tablespoon of oil. Add the tagliatelle, a third at a time to keep the water on the boil and push down under the water as it softens. Cook until just tender for 12-15 minutes and then drain.

Place the cheeses and the cream into a saucepan, heat until the cream is boiling and then pour it over the pasta, stirring until it is coated with the cheese. Season to taste and serve.

As Tagliatelle with Three Cheeses is very rich, you eat less of it than other pasta dishes.

PRAWNS WITH ALMOND GARLIC BUTTER

When you buy prawns for this dish select large ones and as much the same size as possible. Often, rather than buying by weight, it is best to buy so many per person.

1 kg (2 lb) green prawns in the shell

pepper

Almond Garlic Butter

2 teaspoons lemon juice

125 g (4 oz) butter

45 g (1½ oz) ground almonds

3 tablespoons finely chopped parsley

1 large clove garlic, crushed

Remove the butter from the refrigerator, chop it into tiny pieces and place these on a plate so they will soften quickly. If you have a food processor there is no need to soften the butter.

Remove the heads from the prawns and pull the legs away. Cut the prawns in half through the centre, between the leg section but cut only to the shell, not through it. Turn the prawns over and using a rolling pin bang gently to flatten them. Turn them over again and pull away the intestinal cord which can now easily be seen.

Almond Garlic Butter

Cream the butter with the parsley, garlic, pepper, lemon juice and almonds. Spread a layer of the butter over the flesh of each prawn, dipping a knife into hot water as you do each one. Refrigerate if not using them immediately.

Place the prawns, butter side up, on a flat tray which will fit under the griller (broiler), and grill them until the butter has melted and the prawns are cooked through. They don't take long because they are quite thin and must not be overcooked. Depending on the heat of the griller, about 5 to 7 minutes should be sufficient time. Serve them instantly. The flesh is quite easy to remove from the shell with a knife and fork.

PLATTER OF FIGS & GRAPES, WALNUTS & CHOCOLATE

8 ripe fresh eating figs

walnuts in the shell

grapes

chocolate wafers

Chill the figs and grapes. Place them on the platter with walnuts in a heap on one side and the chocolate wafers on the other.

SPIKED COFFEE

4 cups (1 litre) strong coffee

⅓ cup (2½ fl oz) Cognac

2 teaspoons sugar

8 tablespoons whipped cream

½ teaspoon almond essence

Mix the coffee with the sugar and almond essence. Be cautious with almond essence, a little is very good in the coffee but too much can spoil it. Add the Cognac and pour the coffee instantly into heated cups or Irish coffee mugs. Top with the cream.

AutumN

MENU
DINNER *Serves 4*

Livers with Hot Vinaigrette Sauce

*Racks of Lamb
with Spiced Tomato Sauce*

Bananas in Sultana & Rum

*Suggested Accompaniments
Sautéed zucchini (15 mins – p. 99)
or
Boiled potatoes (20 mins)
or
Crispy zucchini strips (5 mins – p. 100)*

Order of Preparation

1. Select about 8 of the best spinach leaves and cover with water to soak them and remove any grit.

2. Prepare the racks of lamb ready for baking and then make the sauce.

3. Make up the sultana and rum mixture for cooking the bananas but don't slice the bananas until just before you cook them.

4. Trim the livers and set out the ingredients for the vinaigrette.

The most exotic breakfast I have ever eaten was in San Francisco, although I admit it would not have suited everybody's taste.

I was about to leave the city to return to Australia when the chef along with the President of Stanford Court Hotel invited me to try one of the specialities of the house: 'Duck Livers with Vinaigrette Sauce'. The only time we could all manage to meet was at 7 o'clock in the morning.

There was orange juice, duck livers accompanied by a bottle of champagne, and to follow, strawberries dipped in sour cream and sugar. Since then I have served and eaten livers in a vinaigrette sauce many times, but as a first course rather than breakfast. Although rich, the vinegar cuts through the fat of the liver and makes it easier to digest. One of the secrets of this dish is to keep the serving small, a little is delicious but too large a portion is overwhelming. You can buy duck livers at many poultry shops or markets. If they are particularly large, four livers may be sufficient. Chicken livers, although not quite as good, could be used instead. Keep the livers pink in the centre. If they are brown throughout, they will be dry.

This is followed by baby racks of lamb with a tomato sauce which is spiced with a little chilli. The sauce can be also be served with grilled lamb chops.

I usually use rum in the banana dessert, and brandy is also good. But don't use a liqueur such as Curaçao or Kirsch as these are very sweet and would make the syrup sickly. If you do wish to use a sweet liqueur, decrease the quantity of golden syrup.

LIVERS WITH HOT VINAIGRETTE SAUCE

---

*8 spinach leaves,
or more if they are small*

8 duck livers (or chicken livers)

90 g (3 oz) butter

*2 tablespoons finely diced
onion*

2 tablespoons red wine vinegar

salt and pepper

2 tablespoons finely chopped chives

Select the spinach, there should be enough to cover the base of the plate on which the livers will be served. A small-sized dinner plate or large bread and butter plate would be ideal. Remove the tough stalk from the spinach and wash well. Then chill the spinach to make it crisp until ready to serve.

Trim the livers of any veins and keep covered in the refrigerator.

Melt 45 g of the butter in a frying pan and add the onion. Cook over high heat for 2 to 3 minutes or until the onion has slightly softened. Then add the livers and cook for just a few minutes, turning them often. They should be slightly pink in the centre, never well done. Add the remaining butter, cut into several pieces and shake the pan to melt it quickly. Add the vinegar, salt, pepper and chives.

Have the spinach-lined plates ready. Spoon the livers onto them and serve immediately.

RACKS OF LAMB WITH SPICED TOMATO SAUCE

A rack of lamb cooks very quickly and is easy to serve. Three cutlets joined together is a good size per portion. When you order these already cut from the butcher, request that the bones are trimmed of fat. The tomato sauce will keep, covered, in the refrigerator for 24 hours.

4 racks of baby lamb

salt and pepper

1 large clove garlic or 2 small cloves, peeled

Sauce

500 g (1 lb) tomatoes

1 medium-sized white onion

1 clove garlic, crushed

about 6 whole peppercorns

¼ teaspoon salt

1 small dried chilli

2 tablespoons white vinegar

2 tablespoons sugar

Using the point of a sharp knife, score the fat in a diamond pattern. Season both sides with salt and pepper. Turn the rack over so the bones are towards you and make a small deep cut between each bone. Cut the garlic into slivers and insert one into each cut. Wrap a piece of foil around the exposed bone.

Place the lamb in a moderate oven, 180°C (350°F/Gas 4) and cook, directly on the rack with a tray underneath to catch the fat which will drip away. This allows the heat to circulate more evenly than when standing in a dish. Cook for about 25 minutes, though the exact timing is determined by the thickness and size of the lamb. They are nicest if still slightly pink in the centre. If you are not sure whether they are ready, remove one and insert the point of a knife into the centre to check. If the juices run pink it will be underdone, if clear, well done. Once cooked they are best served immediately. If you want to keep them aside for a few minutes, remove and wrap in foil — they will retain heat, but also tend to continue cooking.

Sauce

Cut the tomatoes in half, then place the flat side down and cut into small dice. Place in a saucepan and keep the heat low while you add the remaining ingredients. Dice the onion finely and add with the garlic, peppercorns, salt, chilli, vinegar and sugar. Stir for a couple of minutes over the heat, then cover the saucepan and cook gently for approximately 20 minutes until all the ingredients have softened completely. Sieve this mixture, pressing down to extract as much pulp as possible. If the tomato and onion have softened to the correct extent this only takes a moment. Taste for seasoning: it should be slightly hot and spicy. If the sauce is too thin, return to the saucepan and cook uncovered for a couple of minutes until it thickens. If too thick, add a spoonful of chicken stock.

Carve the cutlets, dividing into the 3 chops. Place a spoonful of the sauce on a heated plate and arrange the cutlets overlapping on this.

BANANAS IN SULTANA & RUM SAUCE

60 g (2 oz) sultanas

¼ cup (2 fl oz) brown rum

3 tablespoons golden syrup (light corn syrup)

3 tablespoons lemon juice

45 g (1½ oz) unsalted butter

4 bananas

Place the sultanas, rum, golden syrup, lemon juice and butter in a small saucepan. Cook until the mixture has come to the boil and the butter has melted.

While the sauce is heating, peel and slice the bananas in half lengthwise. Place the halves in a shallow, ovenproof dish. They may either overlap or form two layers. Pour the sauce over the top of the bananas.

Cover, either with a lid or a seal of foil and bake in a moderate oven, 180°C (350°F/Gas 4) for about 12 to 15 minutes or until the bananas are slightly soft. Serve this directly from the dish with vanilla ice cream.

AutumN

MENU
DINNER *Serves 4*

Smoked Salmon Spread with Toast

Fillet Steak with Red Wine Sauce

Orange Sabayon & Fruit

Suggested Accompaniments
Mixed green salad with celery
& fennel
or
Potato cubes with garlic
& parsley (20 mins – p. 95)
or
Beans with Kaiser Fleisch (12 mins –
p. 89)

Order of Preparation
1. Prepare Salmon Spread and chill.

2. If serving fruit with the Orange Sabayon, prepare this and refrigerate.

3. Trim the steak and get the sauce ingredients ready.

4. Make the Orange Sabayon.

In the middle of the eighteenth century, salmon was smoked and sold as a delicacy in Russia, mainly to Jewish families. Later that century, one of the first commercial enterprises was founded in London. In the beginning most of the trade was still for the Jewish community, but then as it became well-known the popularity of the fish increased. It is still rated as one of the most popular of all luxury foods, but is now exorbitantly expensive. The ready packaged salmon is quite salty, but is perfectly adequate to use for this spread.

The recipe makes only a small amount of spread but it is sufficient for four people. Place it in small individual containers, one for each person and accompany with toast triangles or toast fingers, rather as you would serve a pâté.

I have used it to coat small pieces of smoked trout and then placed the trout on bread and butter for an appetizer. It is also wonderful spooned over an omelette and served as a luncheon dish.

Steak with Red Wine Sauce is best when made with fillet steak, but if you prefer you could use another cut of grilling steak. There isn't a lot of sauce but it gives an intense flavour to the meat – and it is meant to be thin, like a juice.

The Orange Sabayon is a French version of Zabaglione, the frothy Italian egg sauce made with Marsala, and although it only takes a few minutes to make must be beaten continuously. As the egg yolks thicken the mixture, it becomes frothy. If it is cooked too quickly and not beaten really well, it will resemble more of a thick orange custard. Use a small hand-held electric beater if you have one, otherwise use a whisk or hand beater.

The Orange Sabayon, chilled and mixed with a few spoonfuls of stiffly whipped cream also makes a wonderful filling for a cake.

SMOKED SALMON SPREAD

It is important when you make this that you buy a thick sour cream. The thin ones will make the spread more of a dip which runs off the toast instead of sitting firmly on top.

Although it can be made and eaten immediately it keeps perfectly well for 12 hours.

½ cup (4 fl oz) thick sour cream

2 teaspoons grated white onion

1 teaspoon horse-radish relish

2 tablespoons mayonnaise

pepper

90 g (3 oz) smoked salmon

Place the cream into a small basin and mix in the onion, horse-radish, mayonnaise and pepper. Don't add salt as the salmon is usually quite salty.

Chop the smoked salmon into small pieces and mix through the cream. Cover and chill as it should be served quite cold.

FILLET STEAK WITH RED WINE SAUCE

4 thick pieces fillet steak	*½ cup (4 fl oz) red wine*
vegetable oil	*salt and pepper*
Sauce	*1 clove garlic, crushed*
1 small white onion	*2 tablespoons finely chopped parsley*
45 g (1½ oz) butter	

Trim the fillet steak of any outside skin. Press down gently on the meat with your hand, it will flatten the steak just slighty and make it a larger round in appearance. Pour just enough vegetable oil into a frying pan to moisten the base and heat. When smoking, place the fillets into the pan and cook over high heat, turning until very brown on both sides. Turn the heat down slightly and continue cooking until done. Timing obviously depends on the thickness and size of the meat and whether you like it rare or medium. Each side should only take a few minutes.

Sauce

The sauce cannot be made until the meat is ready as the same pan is used, this gives much more flavour as it picks up the colour and taste from the meat.

Prepare the ingredients for the sauce while the steak is cooking. Dice the onion very finely so it will only take a moment to cook.

Transfer the meat to a heated platter, cover and leave in a warm place while making the sauce. Pour out any oil remaining in the pan. Add the finely diced onion and fry for a moment, stirring continually. It will cook quickly. When the onion darkens in colour add the butter, stirring until it melts.

Add the red wine, a little salt and pepper and the garlic. Turn up the heat and cook rapidly for a couple of minutes or until the sauce has reduced by about half. Lastly add the parsley, stir and remove immediately from the heat. If there are any juices on the plate with the meat these can also be added to the sauce.

Place the steaks in the pan, turning to moisten them. Serve on dinner plates, dividing a little sauce between them, and spooning it over the meat.

ORANGE SABAYON

The sauce is served with any fresh fruits in season, slices of orange, slices of pear, strawberries etc. It can be used as a sauce over ice cream but this makes a very sweet dessert.

3 egg yolks	*2 tablespoons Grand Marnier*
2 tablespoons caster (powdered) sugar	*1 tablespoon brandy*

Place a saucepan half-filled with water on to boil. Place the egg yolks, sugar, Grand Marnier and brandy into a china or glass bowl and whisk to mix. Stand this in the pan of water, the water should be level with the egg mixture. Whisk or beat as it warms through and it will become fluffy, pale in colour and thick. It takes approximately 5 minutes.

Remove the bowl from the pan and continue beating for another minute so that the mixture doesn't set on the sides of the dish.

Leave aside to cool, or you can serve it immediately. If the egg yolks were properly thickened it will remain fluffy for several hours. As it is very rich only a little is served, spooned over sliced fruits in individual dishes.

AutumN

MENU

DINNER *Serves 4*

Sautéed Tomatoes with Spiced Dressing

Roasted Pepper Steak with Pimento & Onion

Pears with Ginger Syllabub

Suggested Accompaniment Tiny boiled potatoes (20 mins)

Order of Preparation
1. Prepare the steak ready for baking.

2. Completely prepare the tomatoes and cover with dressing. Set them aside at room temperature.

3. Cook the pimento and onion accompaniment.

4. Make the syllabub and chill, but leave the preparation of the pears until the dessert is served.

This first course is a salad of tomatoes which have first been cooked in oil. They shouldn't become really soft, just tender on the outside to enable them to absorb the flavouring of the dressing. While it is best to use ripe tomatoes with a good flavour, it is possible to make this quite successfully with firm tomatoes. Even those which normally wouldn't make a good salad will taste good in this recipe.

The main dish uses rump steak but it is roasted rather than being grilled or sautéed. Although the peppers on top are quite hot, they form a coating on only one side of the meat; if they covered it you would use much less. The timing I have given can only be regarded as approximate for this dish; it depends upon the thickness of the meat. You must use your own judgement on this and if you are in a hurry, buy a thin long piece instead of a chunky section.

Syllabub is one of the nicest of old English desserts, light and fresh despite the large quantities of cream used in the recipe. Originally made by milking the cow directly into the bowl, later recipes instructed one to stand on a high stool and pour fresh milk into a container on the floor to achieve the same result. You can serve plain syllabub over any fruit; in this syllabub the added ginger makes it best of all with pears. It is also good served by itself with small biscuits.

SAUTÉED TOMATOES WITH SPICED DRESSING

4 medium-sized tomatoes

2 tablespoons vegetable or olive oil

salt and pepper

sugar

Dressing

5 tablespoons vegetable or olive oil

2 tablespoons white wine vinegar

1 tablespoon finely chopped gherkin (see Note)

1 tablespoon capers, finely chopped

1 clove garlic, crushed

pinch salt

black pepper

Trim both ends from the tomatoes. Cut them in half. Heat the oil in a large frying pan and add the tomatoes. You will probably find you need to do this in two batches unless the pan is particularly large. When the tomatoes have softened on one side, turn them over and cook for a moment on the other side. Only the outside layers should be cooked, the tomatoes should not be too soft. Place them on a serving platter and while warm, season with salt and pepper and sprinkle a pinch of sugar on top of each half.

Dressing
Place the oil in a small basin, add the vinegar and whisk for a minute with a fork. Mix in the gherkin, capers, garlic, salt and pepper. Pour over the still warm tomatoes and leave aside to cool. Do not refrigerate, the flavour is much better if the tomatoes are at room temperature. Serve with lots of crusty bread or brown bread and butter wedges.

Note: Since gherkins are time-consuming to chop, substitute a tablespoon of gherkin spread or gherkin relish if you prefer.

Sautéed Tomatoes with Spiced Dressing
Roasted Pepper Steak with Pimento and Onion
Pears with Ginger Syllabub
(see p. 54)

AUTUMN

Avocado & Curried Mushroom Quiche without a crust
Oranges in Rosewater Sauce
(see p. 44)

AutumN

ROASTED PEPPER STEAK

1 thick piece of rump steak weighing 750 g-1 kg (1½-2 lb) depending upon appetites

oil

1 tablespoon green peppercorns

2 tablespoons French or Dijon mustard

black pepper

Pre-heat the oven to 200°C (400°F/Gas 6). Place a baking dish in the oven to heat.
   Trim away all the fat from the top of the steak. Brush the meat lightly with oil.
   Crush the green peppercorns with the back of a knife and spread in a layer over one side of the meat, then spread the mustard on top of this. Grind enough black pepper to make a light coating which sticks to the top of the mustard.
   Place the meat on the preheated dish and bake for about 25 minutes for 750 g beef, or 35 minutes for 1 kg beef for a medium steak. However, the timing can vary according to the thickness of the steak. When ready, remove from the oven, cover lightly with foil and stand for 5 minutes or even 10 minutes before slicing. This makes it easier to slice the meat more evenly and it will not lose its juices as much when cut. Cut in thin slices and place them, slightly overlapping, on heated plates. Serve with Pimento and Onion. Leftover meat is excellent with salad.

PIMENTO AND ONION

3 large onions

45 g (1½ oz) butter

1 tablespoon vegetable oil

155 g (5 oz) canned pimento

salt and pepper

Peel the onions and cut in half. Place them, cut-side down, on a board and cut into thin slices. Heat the butter and oil together in a saucepan and add the onions. Cook, stirring for about 5 minutes to coat them with the butter, then leave to sauté gently for another 10 minutes. If they have not softened, cover the pan and leave them to 'sweat'. But watch that they don't become brown.
   While they are cooking, drain the pimentoes, discard the liquid in the can and cut them into small dice. Add to the onions with salt and pepper. After the beef has stood for a short time before carving you will find that there is often some juice around it. Pour this into the onions and mix it through. The onion and pimento can be kept warm for some time without spoiling.

PEARS WITH GINGER SYLLABUB

½ cup (4 fl oz) thick cream

2 tablespoons caster (powdered) sugar

1 tablespoon lemon juice

2 tablespoons finely chopped glacé or crystallised ginger

pinch ginger

pinch nutmeg

3 tablespoons dry white wine

500 g (1 lb) ripe eating pears

Whip the cream until it is stiff. Mix the sugar, lemon juice, ginger, cinnamon, nutmeg and wine together in a small bowl and stir. Gradually mix this into the cream, whisking. It should form soft peaks. Cover the mixture and chill. Peel the pears and cut them into quarters, then core. Cut into thin slices or small dice and arrange them in glasses or individual dessert dishes. Spoon the ginger syllabub over the top and serve immediately.

MENU

AUTUMN DINNER *Serves 4*

Mushrooms with Cream & Parsley

Chicken Breasts
with Orange & Almond Sauce

Chocolate Soufflé Omelette

Suggested Accompaniments
Boiled baby potatoes *(20 mins)*
or
Mixed green salad

Order of Preparation
1. Prepare the chicken breasts and leave aside to cook in the casserole.

2. Set out and measure ingredients for the Soufflé Omelette.

3. Trim and cook the mushrooms.

There is often disagreement as to the handling of mushrooms. Should they be peeled? Should they be washed? I find the best flavour of all is next to the skin and the only soil is at the base of the stem where it came in contact with the growing compound. It hardly seems necessary to wash them, especially since they absorb water like a sponge, and when heated, expel this water into the dish, changing the flavouring of the sauce or altering the consistency. If they look a bit dirty, wipe them over with a clean damp cloth or paper towel.

The mushroom dish, served as a first course is simple and the addition of cream, while hardly noticeable in the finished dish, gives it a rich taste. I use button mushrooms for this as they are lighter, but for a stronger flavour leave your mushrooms in the refrigerator until they have opened a little and darkened slightly.

The chicken dish is made with chicken breasts, but you could use chicken portions. However they would need longer cooking and must be covered when baked with the sauce in the oven.

The chocolate dessert resembles a soufflé in texture but for the sake of speed, is made in a pan as you would make an omelette. It is first partly cooked on top of the stove and then placed under a pre-heated griller (broiler) to puff up the top. Although any good heavy frying pan could be used, this is easiest to make with a non-stick pan. You can use a small pan of 20 cm (8 in) diameter and then the omelette would be turned out flat and broken into four sections for serving. You can also make a large omelette in a huge pan, it will be flatter but can then be folded in half and cut into wedges to serve.

One of the most important things to remember with soufflé omelettes is that unlike French omelettes they cannot be cooked quickly over high heat. The mixture must cook slowly so that the base browns without burning and the centre is cooked through. I have specified unsalted butter. Salted butter tastes quite strong in the soufflé omelette and spoils the flavour.

Serve it with cream or ice cream. For a very rich dessert, spoon a little chocolate sauce over the soufflé omelette and ice cream.

MUSHROOMS WITH CREAM & PARSLEY

500 g (1 lb) small button mushrooms

60 g (2 oz) butter

salt and pepper

2 tablespoons thick cream

2 tablespoons finely chopped parsley

1 teaspoon lemon juice

Cut the stalks of the mushrooms level with the caps. Melt the butter and add the mushrooms. Season as they cook with some salt and pepper. Keep the heat high so the mushrooms will not stew but will fry quickly. When they have absorbed all the butter, add the cream and leave to cook, still over a high heat, until they are just softened. No liquid should be left in the pan, just a creamy coating around the mushrooms. Add the parsley and lemon juice and mix through. Serve with hot toast fingers.

Note: The mushrooms can be prepared, cooked beforehand and then reheated. While they still taste delicious using this method, some of the firmness of the mushrooms will be lost and they will be quite soft.

CHICKEN BREASTS WITH ORANGE & ALMOND SAUCE

4 chicken breasts	grated rind of 1 orange
flour	¼ cup (2 fl oz) chicken stock
salt and pepper	1 teaspoon redcurrant jelly
45 g (1½ oz) butter	salt and pepper
¼ cup (2 fl oz) orange juice	2 tablespoons almond flakes

Dust the chicken breasts with flour which has been seasoned with salt and pepper. Melt the butter in a frying pan and cook the chicken breasts, turning until they have changed colour. They will still be raw inside. Transfer them to a shallow ovenproof dish placing them in one layer.

Mix together in a basin the orange juice, rind, chicken stock and red currant jelly. Wipe out the frying pan, add the orange mixture and bring to the boil. Cook for a moment until the red currant jelly has dissolved. Season. Pour this sauce over the chicken breasts and place in a moderate oven, 180°C (350°F/Gas 4) for about 15 minutes or until the chicken is quite tender. While the chicken is cooking, place the almond flakes on a dry baking tray and cook in the oven until toasted. Watch them, as they will overcook and become bitter if left too long. You can also cook the almond flakes in a frying pan that has a piece of butter the size of a pea placed in it to moisten the almonds. Cook the almonds in the pan, shaking, until golden. Leave to drain on paper.

Place a chicken breast on each plate and scatter a few almonds on top of each one. If you prefer you could serve the dish directly from the oven: just scatter the almonds over the top before taking it to the table.

CHOCOLATE SOUFFLÉ OMELETTE

3 egg yolks	3 egg whites
2 tablespoons caster (powdered) sugar	pinch salt
2 tablespoons cocoa	15 g (½ oz) unsalted butter
1 tablespoon brandy	

Preheat the griller (broiler). Place the egg yolks, caster sugar and cocoa into a bowl and beat for a minute until thick. Mix in the brandy. Beat the egg whites with the pinch of salt in a separate bowl until stiff. Place the butter on to melt in a frying pan. Gently fold the egg whites into the yolks, one-third at a time. As soon as the butter has melted, pour in the omelette mixture and shake gently for a moment so that it spreads out evenly. Cook over medium heat for 4 to 5 minutes. When the base is well set, place the pan underneath the griller and cook for a minute until the top has puffed and is just firm to touch. Turn the omelette out by tilting it onto a plate. Dust some icing sugar over the top if you wish. Serve instantly, with cream or ice cream.

AUTUMN

MENU

DINNER *Serves 4*

Mushroom Salad with Walnut Dressing

Chicken on a Bed of Peas & Ham

Pears in Passionfruit Sauce

Suggested Accompaniments
Tiny boiled potatoes *(20 mins)*
or
Baked potato slices *(30 mins – p. 94)*
or
Garlic-scented tomatoes *(15 mins – p. 99)*

Order of Preparation
1. Cook the peas and prepare the chicken.

2. Place the pears into the saucepan with the sauce and leave them gently cooking.

3. Make up the mushroom salad.

Walnut and hazelnut oil have become the luxury oils to use in the new style of salad dishes. Rich in flavour, these are mainly used when the course is to be served on its own rather than as an accompaniment. They are expensive and the top quality ones are difficult to buy. The dressing for the mushroom salad uses a vegetable oil but the addition of walnuts gives it a lovely texture and flavour. You can use shelled walnuts in a packet, but if you have time, shell them yourself. Only a little is needed and when fresh they lend more flavour. The same dressing makes an interesting change on a salad of lettuce or baby spinach leaves.

The main dish of chicken breasts is served on a bed of peas and ham. The addition of just a few extra seasonings such as the parsley, nutmeg and cream makes a big difference to the taste of freeze dried peas. You can use chicken portions instead of breasts for the dish, it takes longer but the flavour will be richer. Prepare the portions by browning them in the same way as the breasts and then when the peas and ham are ready, place the chicken portions on top, cover the casserole and cook for 25 minutes. The dish can be made beforehand and reheated but it must be well covered or it will become dry.

The tang of passionfruit combined with orange and pears in the dessert is perfect. And although the dessert contains cream and follows a creamy main course, the textures are completely different.

MUSHROOM SALAD WITH WALNUT DRESSING

250 g (8 oz) small, very firm mushrooms

6 tablespoons vegetable oil

2 tablespoons white wine vinegar

2 teaspoons French mustard

2 teaspoons horse-radish relish

3 tablespoons finely chopped walnuts

salt and pepper

Wipe the tops of the mushrooms or wash them if you feel it is necessary (I prefer not to rinse them as it makes them wet in the salad). Remove the stalks — if they are small just cut them level with the caps. Cut the mushrooms into thin slices.

Mix together the oil and vinegar, whisking. Add the mustard, horse-radish relish and walnuts. Season. Keep the dressing and mushrooms separate until about 10 minutes before serving. Add the dressing to the mushrooms, turning them over gently to coat.

You can serve this on a lettuce leaf if you wish or else make a small mound on a plate. It has a lovely fresh light flavour.

CHICKEN ON A BED OF PEAS & HAM

Peas and Ham

45 g (1½ oz) packet of freeze-dried peas

2 cups (16 fl oz) water

45 g (1½ oz) butter

1 teaspoon sugar

2 tablespoons roughly chopped parsley

pinch grated nutmeg

1 teaspoon salt

1 teaspoon flour

¼ cup (2 fl oz) thick cream

125 g (4 oz) ham

Chicken Breasts

4 chicken breasts

flour

salt and pepper

45 g (1½ oz) butter

Peas and Ham

Place the peas and the water in a saucepan, add the butter, sugar, parsley, nutmeg and salt and bring to the boil. Simmer gently until the peas are quite tender. If the liquid evaporates too much, cover the saucepan. Mix the flour and cream together. Cut the ham into small dice. When the peas are tender there should be just enough liquid to barely cover them. If there is a lot, boil rapidly to reduce it. Add the cream and flour and stir until it comes to the boil and thickens. Mix the ham into the peas and place in a shallow casserole. It should be large enough to allow the 4 chicken breasts to rest on top in one layer.

Chicken Breasts

Dip the chicken breasts into the flour which has been seasoned with salt and pepper. Heat the butter in a frying pan, add the chicken breasts and cook until the outsides have browned. They will remain undercooked in the centre. Place the chicken breasts on top of the bed of peas, moisten with a little of the butter from the frying pan, and cook in a moderate oven, 180°C (350°F/Gas 4) for 10 to 15 minutes or until they are cooked through. If the peas start to look dry, cover the top with foil for the last 5 minutes of cooking. Serve the chicken breasts with a spoonful of the creamy peas and ham around them.

PEARS IN PASSIONFRUIT SAUCE

When you buy the pears for this, choose those which are beginning to ripen; very hard green pears take a long time to cook.

⅓ cup (3 oz) sugar

1 cup (8 fl oz) water

about 8 strips of orange rind

½ cup (4 fl oz) fresh orange juice

4 pears

¼ cup (2 fl oz) thick cream

2 passionfruit

Place the sugar, water, orange rind and juice into a saucepan and heat. While this is warming, peel the pears and core them. Cut each pear into about 8 pieces. Place into the liquid and cook, without a lid, for about 10 minutes, turning the fruit around in the syrup occasionally. Then place a lid on the pan and cook them until tender.

Remove the lid, add the cream, turn up the heat and boil rapidly until the juices are rather glazed and slightly thickened. Remove from the heat, cut the passionfruit into half and add the pulp to the saucepan. Place in a bowl to cool. Remove the orange rind. Serve warm just as it is or with some small biscuits.

Note: This dessert could be eaten chilled, but when cold the sauce becomes rather thick and a little buttery.

WinteR

MENU
LUNCH *Serves 4*

Eggs New Orleans Style

Orange Gratin

Suggested Accompaniments
Hot buttered toast fingers
Small green salad to be served
after the eggs

Order of Preparation
1. Completely prepare the egg dish ready for the oven.

2. Prepare the orange gratin and refrigerate, the topping must be prepared at the last moment.

New Orleans is one of the most interesting and food-conscious cities in the United States, its French influence mixed with the spiciness of Spain, a legacy from the years of Spanish domination.

While you can eat brunch in most cities in America, in New Orleans the occasion has become a local institution, featuring dishes traditional to the area.

You commence the day with an 'eye opener', such as a deceptively mild-tasting New Orleans gin fizz, mint julep or salzerac. The brunch follows with perhaps soup, oysters, baby quail, which are a favourite, or exotic egg dishes. Apart from the more familiar such as 'Eggs Benedict', 'Eggs Florentine' and omelettes, each restaurant will have specialities of their own. This egg dish is not from one particular place but typifies the style of dish often served and it makes an unusual but perfect lunch dish.

It is important to keep a watchful eye on the eggs, they tend to change rather quickly from raw eggs to very hard and are nicest still soft. Although I prefer hot buttered toast you can serve some crusty bread instead if it is easier.

I like the combination of red wine mixed with the mushrooms and ham but if you have some white wine open you could use this instead. The flavour, naturally is different, not quite as rich, but still good.

The Orange Gratin could be made with other fruits at other times of the year. For example when strawberries, raspberries or nectarines are in season, any of these can be placed in the base of the gratin dish and topped with the cream. I use orange liqueur with the oranges but with other fruits you could use something different such as Kirsch, brandy or cognac, depending on the fruits and your own personal preference.

It is important to watch the gratin under the griller as it bakes; leaving it for even a few minutes could mean one section browns too much, and as the sugar heats like toffee, it can burn.

EGGS NEW ORLEANS STYLE

45 g (1½ oz) butter	*½ cup (4 fl oz) red wine*
1 onion, finely diced	*salt and pepper*
125 g (4 oz) mushrooms	*8 eggs*
125 g (4 oz) ham	*4 tablespoons thick cream*
2 teaspoons flour	

Melt the butter in a frying pan and add the onion. Sauté, stirring occasionally until the onion has slightly softened. While the onion is cooking, cut the stalks of the mushrooms level with the caps and slice the mushrooms thinly. Add these to the pan. Dice the ham finely and add.

Mix in the flour, add the wine and stir until it comes to the boil and thickens. Cook for a couple of minutes until it has reduced to about 2 tablespoons. Season to taste.

Divide this mixture between four small individual ovenproof casseroles. You can use oblong dishes or soufflé dishes, the shape is immaterial but they need to have a capacity of 1 cup (8 fl oz). Break two eggs on top of the mixture in each dish and season them.

Trickle a tablespoon of cream over the eggs and cover them with foil (otherwise they will dry on top). Bake in a moderate oven, 180°C (350°F/Gas 4) for about 15 minutes or until the eggs have just set. Timing will vary, according to the size of the dishes, but you need to watch these as the eggs should not be hard, just lightly set on top.

Serve them at the table in the dish in which they were cooked.

ORANGE GRATIN

4 oranges	*1 cup (8 fl oz) thick cream*
2 tablespoons orange-flavoured liqueur	*caster (powdered) sugar*

Cut the top and bottom from each orange. Peel and trim away all the white pith. Cut each orange in half and then placing the cut side on a board, cut into thin slices. If there are pips in the orange, flick them out as you slice the fruit. Arrange in a shallow ovenproof china or glass dish, approximately 20 cm (8 in) in diameter. Pour the liqueur over the top.

Beat the cream until it holds its shape; don't overbeat. Spread in a layer over the oranges and then chill for about 20 minutes.

The finishing touches to this dish must be done just before serving. Sift enough caster sugar over the cream to cover the top quite thickly. Fold a strip of foil around the edge of the dish to prevent it from becoming brown or damaged by the heat. Place under a hot griller (broiler) and cook until the top has formed a marbled, rippled effect of caramel. As the top heats, the cream melts so that instead of the sugar caramelising in one layer it bubbles into the cream. It should all be quite melted and golden, but if any sugary pieces remain on top, turn the dish around until they melt. Remove and leave to settle for about a minute, then serve, spooning on to dessert plates which have a raised edge as there is quite a bit of sauce with this. Small gratin dishes enable you to serve individual Orange Gratins, but it is still important to grill and cook them evenly.

MENU

WINTER

LUNCH   *Serves 4*

Teriyaki Hamburgers

Zucchini & Onion Salad

Apples Baked in Cointreau

Order of Preparation
1. Prepare the apple dish and place in the oven to cook.

2. Prepare the hamburgers.

3. Grate the zucchini and cook the onion. Make up the dressing.

It may be their national dish but the Americans didn't invent the hamburger, it was a popular main dish in Germany centuries before it was heard of in the United States. However the Americans were the first to place the meat between a bun enabling the dish to be eaten with the hands. A hamburger can be quite a simple dish or as elaborate as you wish, with the addition of onions, spices, wine, capers, anchovies etc. added to the meat — but not all together. The spices added to the Teriyaki hamburger, which is a regular feature on menus in Hawaii, make it even more juicy and moist than usual.

I found that when making a Teriyaki hamburger, if some of the sauce was added to the meat, and some kept aside to be poured over when it was cooked, a glorious glaze and flavour cooked on the outside. Perfect for lunch, a salad could be served with this and if you have time, thin straw potatoes are also good. I like to serve a fruit dessert after this. There is not a great choice in winter, but apples are always easily obtainable. They are baked with a liqueur, Cointreau is used in this recipe but other liqueurs could go into the dish instead. Try Kirsch, Calvados, Curaçao or brandy. It won't have a strong flavour, but will give a wonderful aroma and flavour to the fruit. It can be made beforehand, left aside and then just gently warmed for a short time while you are eating the meal.

TERIYAKI HAMBURGERS

---

500 g (1 lb) beef, finely minced

1 tablespoon oil

Teriyaki Sauce

1 clove garlic, crushed

1 small white onion, finely chopped

1 teaspoon grated fresh ginger

⅓ cup (2½ fl oz) soy sauce

1 tablespoon sugar

½ teaspoon salt

2 tablespoons dry sherry

Mix together all the ingredients for the Teriyaki sauce in a small basin. Place the meat in a bowl. Mix in half of the Teriyaki sauce and using your hands, gently turn and knead lightly until the meat has absorbed all the liquid. Form into 4 round patties. Heat the oil in a frying pan and when smoking hot, add the hamburgers.

Cook, turning until it is done to the right degree in the centre. I prefer mine very pink but not everybody likes hamburgers underdone. However the longer they are cooked, the drier the meat will become. Drain off any excess oil or fat in the pan.

Mix ½ cup (4 fl oz) water with the reserved Teriyaki sauce and add to the pan. Cook over a high heat until most of the sauce has cooked away, turning the meat over to moisten and pick up flavour. Serve with a little of the sauce on top. It will be quite dark and glazed.

Note: There is not much salt in this recipe because soy sauce is generally quite salty. If you are not certain of the brand you are using, check for saltiness by placing a little on the tip of your tongue. If not very salty, add a little more to the Teriyaki mixture.

ZUCCHINI AND ONION SALAD

1 large or 2 small onions	***Dressing***
1 tablespoon oil	*3 tablespoons oil*
250 g (8 oz) baby zucchini (courgettes)	*1 tablespoon white vinegar*
	1 teaspoon dry, English mustard
	1 teaspoon honey
	salt

Cut the onion in half and then into thin slices. Heat the oil, add the onion and cook it gently, stirring occasionally while you prepare the zucchini. Don't allow the onion to brown. Trim off the ends and grate the zucchini, making the shreds as long as possible. A food processor can be used for this or the coarsest surface of a hand grater. Place the zucchini into a bowl and mix in the softened onion. Set it aside (if you're leaving it for more than 30 minutes, chill it in the refrigerator). Mix all the dressing ingredients together with a fork and set aside. Just before serving, mix the dressing into the zucchini, checking for salt and pepper as zucchini needs to be fairly well seasoned.

APPLES BAKED IN COINTREAU

45 g (1½ oz) unsalted butter	*2 tablespoons sugar*
½ cup orange juice	*3 tablespoons Cointreau*
750 g (1½ lb) Granny Smith apples	

Preheat the oven to 180°C (350°F/Gas 4). Place the butter and orange juice into a casserole which has a tight fitting lid. Heat it in the oven while you prepare the apples. Peel, core and slice the apples thinly. Put them in the casserole, scatter the sugar and 2 tablespoons of the Cointreau over the top. Stir and return the dish to the oven, covered tightly to keep the aroma in. Cook for 25 to 30 minutes or until they are soft. Timing will vary according to the freshness of the apples and the thickness of the slices. Stir them once to make certain they're cooking evenly. When ready, stir in the remaining tablespoon of Cointreau. Serve them hot or warm with running cream.

Note: You can cook the apples beforehand and they can be reheated but this dish must be served warm, not cold or the butter will set in tiny pieces throughout the sauce.

MENU

DINNER   *Serves 4*

Avocado, Bacon & Caviar Appetiser

Split Chicken with Onions

Apple Cream

Suggested Accompaniments
Sautéed zucchini with tomato
(15 mins – p. 100)
or
Sautéed grated zucchini
(5 mins – p. 101)
or
Green salad

Order of Preparation
1. Place chicken into the oven.

2. Prepare the avocado dish but don't add the caviar until just before serving time.

3. Start to make the apple cream.

This first course was one of those creations born of necessity. One evening I suddenly had four guests and one avocado, which despite its size was not sufficient to serve in any way except diced, which didn't seem particularly exciting.

With bacon and caviar it made a very pretty dish and the flavours of the toppings were somehow perfect with the rich, blandness of the avocado. Sometimes, instead of serving this in individual dishes I make a large bowl of the salad and serve it on flat plates as a first course. If you present it this way then don't shred the lettuce finely as you would for individual servings but break enough lettuce into small bite-sized pieces to cover the base of a salad bowl and then top with the avocado, bacon and caviar. Besides tasting good, this dish has the extra advantage of looking stunning.

Chicken, split down the centre for quicker cooking, is mounded over a heap of onions in a baking dish. The onions gain a delicious flavour from the chicken juices. Add a pinch of herbs to the onions or a couple of cloves of unpeeled garlic. Remove the garlic before serving as it won't be quite soft enough to eat but will flavour and perfume the onion.

The apple cream is a cross between a custard and a creamy mixture, a good winter dessert and the dish can be varied by using other fruits.

AVOCADO, BACON & CAVIAR APPETISER

Although one avocado would not usually serve four people, because of the way this is presented, one is ample as a first course.

185 g (6 oz) bacon

1 avocado,
weighing approximately 250 g (8 oz)

1 tablespoon lemon juice

few drops Tabasco sauce

2 tablespoons mayonnaise

pepper

4 lettuce leaves

45 g (1½ oz) pink caviar

Cut the bacon into very small dice or strips and place into a dry frying pan. Cook, stirring occasionally until it is quite crisp. Drain well on kitchen paper.

While this is cooking, cut the avocado in half and twist sideways, it will lift away from the stone and come apart easily, then remove the other side from the stone using the point of a small knife to loosen it. Peel the avocado and cut into dice. Mix the lemon juice with the Tabasco and mayonnaise and season with pepper. Do not use salt as the bacon will supply sufficient. Mix the avocado dice with the sauce, turning to coat it evenly.

Shred the lettuce leaves finely. Place some lettuce in the base of small dishes, or bowls. Top with several spoonfuls of the avocado and then divide the bacon between the dishes. Scatter the pink caviar over the top at the last moment. The dish can be made an hour beforehand, but do not keep it too long or the avocado will spoil.

SPLIT CHICKEN WITH ONIONS

*1 chicken
weighing approximately 1.5 kg (3 lb)*

salt and pepper

45 g (1½ oz butter)

2 large or 3 medium-sized onions

Remove the wing tips from the chicken and cut down the backbone using poultry shears or kitchen scissors. Remove the fat from the tail. Place the chicken down on a board, breast facing towards you and press down firmly with your hands to flatten out the chicken. The entire section of backbone can be trimmed away to make carving easier. Season the chicken generously with salt and pepper.

Place the butter in a small saucepan and leave to melt gently. Peel the onions and cut each in half. Then cut again into segments like an apple, allowing about 8 segments for the large onions, 6 for medium-sized onions. Place the onions in a heap in the centre of a baking dish. Spoon about half the butter over the top, season with salt and pepper. Then place the chicken on top of the onions, breast side upwards and trickle the remainder of the butter over the chicken.

The chicken must completely cover the onions, which will steam in the butter. Any juices which drip down will make the onions moist and flavoursome by the time the chicken is cooked. Place the baking dish in a moderate oven, 180°C (350°F/Gas 4) and cook, basting the chicken several times for 45 to 50 minutes.

Remove the chicken and cut down the centre, then across the leg and thigh, making four large portions. Serve some of the onions alongside each portion of chicken.

APPLE CREAM

The apples are first cooked in the oven for a short time in butter and brown sugar which form a light caramel sauce around them. When the custard mixture is poured over the top it sets quickly. The same dish can be prepared using other fruits such as apricots, peaches and cherries.

250 g (8 oz) cooking apples

30 g (1 oz) unsalted butter

1 tablespoon brown sugar

2 eggs

1 cup (8 fl oz) thick cream

¼ teaspoon vanilla essence

2 tablespoons caster (powdered) sugar

1 tablespoon brandy

cinnamon

Peel and core the apples. Cut them into small dice, rather than slicing them. Place the apples in a china quiche dish or a pie dish with a 3 cup (24 fl oz) capacity. Apple Cream is easiest if served at the table from the dish in which it was cooked.

Cut the butter into a few small pieces and scatter over the top of the apples, then sprinkle over the brown sugar. Bake in a moderate oven, 180°C (350°F/Gas 4) for about 10 minutes, or until the apples have slightly softened.

While the apples are cooking, beat the eggs, cream, vanilla, sugar and brandy together in a small bowl. Pour the mixture over the top of the apples and bake for 15 minutes longer or until the custard is just set in the centre. Remove from the oven and leave it to settle for about five minutes. Sprinkle a very light dusting of cinnamon over the top and serve warm, either plain or with some cream.

WinteR

MENU
DINNER *Serves 4*

Stuffed Mushrooms with Cheese Topping

Pork Chops with Apples & Cider

Nutmeg Mousse

Suggested Accompaniments
Beans with sesame seeds *(12 mins – p. 88)*
or
Sautéed potato cubes *(20 mins – p. 97)*
or
Green salad

Order of Preparation
1. Prepare the pork chops ready for the oven.

2. Make the nutmeg mousse and refrigerate it so that it will be set by the time the first two courses have been eaten.

3. Stuff the mushrooms ready for baking.

Stuffed mushrooms make a perfect first course and are also good as a main course for luncheons, served with a salad.

The variety of ingredients you can use to stuff a mushroom is unending. I find this one extremely popular; the port in the sauce gives the mushrooms a very full flavour. Don't feel you must follow the recipe to the letter, change it and alter the seasonings to suit your mood. Herbs or parsley could be added; sometimes I add a couple of tablespoons of pine nuts to the stuffing mixture, and occasionally I chop a spoonful of walnuts or almonds and mix through. The mushrooms can be covered and left for several hours in the refrigerator before cooking.

Apples and cider have an affinity with pork and help to cut the richness of the meat. Watch the timing on this dish: I have suggested 30 minutes but it will vary according to the thickness of the meat.

The nutmeg mousse for dessert does not require cooking. The raw eggs are beaten with the sugar and the flavour is freshened with lemon juice. It can also be made with other spices such as cinnamon. The dessert is lovely on its own but also good with fruit. For example, poached pears are good with nutmeg mousse, use apples if you make a cinnamon mousse. On its own the mousse serves 4, but when fruit is added it makes 6 servings.

STUFFED MUSHROOMS WITH CHEESE TOPPING

8 large, flat mushrooms, weighing about 60 g (2 oz) each

salt and pepper

30 g (1 oz) butter

1 tablespoon oil

Stuffing

4 large mushrooms

reserved stalks from the 8 mushrooms

30 g (1 oz) butter

1 tablespoon finely chopped onion

1 clove garlic, crushed

salt and pepper

2 tablespoons port

2 tablespoons breadcrumbs, made from stale bread

Gruyère cheese, thinly sliced

Remove the stalks from the mushrooms and reserve. Season the mushrooms with salt and pepper. Melt the butter in a small saucepan, add the oil and brush the tops of the mushrooms with this mixture (this will prevent them from drying out). Place them in 1 layer in a shallow ovenproof dish. It is not necessary to butter it.

Stuffing

Cut the whole mushrooms and their stalks into small dice. Melt the butter, add the mushrooms, onion and garlic and sauté for a few minutes, stirring occasionally until the mushrooms have softened. Season with salt and pepper. Increase the heat, add the port and boil until it has completely evaporated.

Put the mixture into a basin and stir in the breadcrumbs. It should hold together; if it is too moist, add a few more crumbs. Fill the mushroom caps with the stuffing and cut enough thin slices of cheese to cover each mushroom. Bake in a moderate oven, 180°C (350°F/Gas 4) for about 10 minutes or until the cheese has melted and the mushrooms are cooked.

PORK CHOPS WITH APPLES & CIDER

4 pork chops

2 teaspoons oil

salt and pepper

1 large cooking apple

30 g (1 oz) butter

1 cup (8 fl oz) cider

pinch cinnamon

3 tablespoons sultanas

2 strips lemon peel

1 teaspoon cornflour (cornstarch)

2 tablespoons water

Trim the rind from the chops. If there is a great deal of fat on the outside, remove a little of this. Heat the oil in a frying pan and add the chops. Cook them over a high heat, turning until they are brown on both sides. While the chops are browning, peel and core the apple and cut it into thin slices. Remove the chops, drain on kitchen paper and season with salt and pepper. Discard the oil from the pan and wipe it out with kitchen paper. Melt the butter in the pan, add the apple and sauté for a moment, stirring. Add the cider, cinnamon, sultanas and strips of peel and bring to the boil. Arrange the chops in an ovenproof casserole which has a lid. They can overlap slightly but are best in 1 layer. Pour the apple mixture over the top, cover the casserole and bake in a moderate oven, 180°C (350°F/Gas 4), turning them once, until they are tender. Depending more on the thickness of the chops than on their size, this usually takes about 30 minutes. Mix the cornflour with the water in a small basin. Pour the juices from the chops into this, stir well and then return it to the casserole. It should thicken from the heat of the dish, otherwise put the dish back into the oven for a few minutes and shake occasionally, rather than stirring. Remove the lemon rind before serving and spoon some of the apples and sultanas over each portion.

NUTMEG MOUSSE

2 teaspoons gelatine

2 tablespoons water

2 eggs

⅓ cup (3 oz) sugar

2 teaspoons brandy

1 tablespoon lemon juice

½ teaspoon freshly grated nutmeg

½ teaspoon vanilla essence

*½ cup (4 fl oz) cream,
whipped until it holds soft peaks*

Place the gelatine into a cup, add the water and mix together. Place the cup in warm water in a small saucepan and heat until the gelatine has dissolved. While this is heating, beat the eggs and sugar until they are very thick and fluffy. As it is hard to do this by hand and takes too long, use an electric mixer if available. When the gelatine has dissolved, stir the brandy and lemon juice into the cup, then add this mixture to the eggs, beating for 30 seconds. Add the nutmeg, vanilla and cream and fold through.

Place into small individual serving dishes. You can use one large bowl instead, but it will take a little longer to set. In small dishes it will be set in about 35 minutes in the refrigerator.

Note: Covered, this dessert keeps well for 24 hours.

MENU
DINNER *Serves 4*

Scallops with Sweet Mustard Sauce	**Order of Preparation** **1. Put the chicken on to cook.**
Chicken in Garlic Sauce	**2. Make up the sauce for the scallops and chill it.**
Grilled Pears with Rum	**3. Prepare the scallops, clean them and toss in flour.**
Suggested Accompaniments ***Potato & carrot purée** (30 mins – p. 96)* ***or*** ***Sautéed potato cubes** (20 mins – p. 97)* ***or*** ***Mixed green salad***	**4. Peel and slice the pears, leaving them to soak until ready to cook if you wish to do this beforehand. Otherwise they only take a moment to slice and can be instantly cooked.**

With the simple logic that the more dominating the flavour or aroma of a herb, the more therapeutic the value, garlic has come at the top of the list of cures for ailments as disparate as the common cold and leprosy since the time of Hippocrates. Fallacies existed that a bulb worn around the neck would protect the wearer against witches. And hopeful Romans, and later Elizabethans, ate the bulbs in the belief that they were a potent aphrodisiac.

An important flavouring in many dishes, it is not the quantity of garlic used which determines the finished taste, but the way it is handled. In some dishes when crushed raw it may have an explosive pungency but in others, such as this main dish of chicken, it ends up with a gentle, almost buttery flavour. The garlic is digestable and quite sweet to eat. Don't recoil in horror at the thought of using 15 cloves, any less and it won't be tasty enough. This dish can be served immediately, or reheated later.

The scallops served as a first course are cooked quite simply; it is the sauce which adds the interest. It's a little like the mustard sauces served in Scandinavian countries with salmon lax, and I find it good to use as a dip with raw vegetables. Try it with some small raw mushrooms, little flowerets of cauliflower or strips of crispy raw zucchini served with pre-dinner drinks.

Both dishes have a richness which needs fruit to follow. If you have some ripe eating pears you may prefer to serve these with cheese instead of making the dessert. However, although the dessert is hot, it only takes a few moments and the fruit is actually just heated through, giving it a light, fresh flavour. This method of preparing pears can be used for ripe eating peaches. You must peel and grill them at the last moment as they discolour easily. You could use white peaches, but I find the yellow ones most successful.

SCALLOPS WITH SWEET MUSTARD SAUCE

Scallops	***Mustard Sauce***
500 g (1 lb) scallops	*2 teaspoons French mustard*
flour	*1 teaspoon dry, English mustard*
salt and pepper	*2 teaspoons sugar*
2 tablespoons oil	*2 teaspoons white vinegar* *¼ cup (2 fl oz) vegetable oil*
30 g (1 oz) butter	*1 tablespoon finely chopped fresh dill (see Note)*

Mix the mustards and sugar together with the vinegar in a small bowl. Add the oil and whisk with a fork, it will be thick. Add the dill. Remove the coral from the scallops. Place a few spoonfuls of flour with some salt and pepper into a brown paper bag. Add the scallops and, holding the end of the bag firmly, shake it up and down. The scallops will be evenly coated. Tip them into a sieve and shake this over the sink. All the excess flour will fall through.

Heat the oil and butter in a large frying pan. Add the scallops, if they won't all fit without crowding, cook half at a time, keeping the cooked ones warm. Fry over high heat for 3 to 5 minutes, tossing and shaking the pan until the scallops are cooked. The cooking time depends on the size of the scallops but they should still be tender and soft in the centre and are spoilt if overcooked. Remove and drain on kitchen paper.

Serve immediately with a little of the mustard sauce on the side.

Note: If you are unable to obtain fresh dill, don't use dried, instead leave this out of the sauce altogether.

CHICKEN IN GARLIC SAUCE

1 chicken weighing about 1.5 kg (3 lb) cut into portions

30 g (1 oz) butter

1 tablespoon oil

15 whole cloves garlic, unpeeled

1 bay leaf

2 teaspoons rosemary, finely chopped

½ cup (4 fl oz) white wine

Heat the butter and oil and add the chicken portions, a few at a time. Sauté, turning them until they have changed colour and transfer them as they cook to an ovenproof casserole with a tight-fitting lid. Season all the chicken pieces with salt and pepper.

Drain off most of the oil from the pan, add the garlic, cook for 1 minute, shaking and then add the bay leaf, rosemary and wine. Tip this mixture over the chicken and bake in a moderate oven, 180°C (350°F/Gas 4) for approximately 35 to 40 minutes or until the chicken is cooked.

Remove the chicken portions and pour the sauce through a sieve. Press down gently on the garlic which will be quite soft. If the sauce looks too thin, boil it over high heat to reduce it.

Serve the chicken with a small spoonful of garlic sauce on top.

GRILLED PEARS WITH RUM

The pears are not actually cooked by this method, just heated through. It is important that you use ripe eating pears, hard ones remain hard even after being heated for some time. Instead of the rum, you can use an orange-flavoured liqueur or brandy but rum tastes remarkably good with pears.

4 ripe eating pears

45 g (1½ oz) unsalted butter

1 tablespoon brown sugar

1 tablespoon white sugar

2 tablespoons brown rum

Peel the pears, core them and cut into slices. If you are not grilling them immediately, place the slices into a bowl of water which has a little lemon juice added so that they won't discolour. Be sure to drain them well before using. Place the pears into a shallow ovenproof dish and dot the butter in small pieces over the top. Scatter the two sugars over this and place under a preheated griller (broiler) for 4 to 5 minutes or until the pears are hot and the sauce formed around them is bubbling. Sprinkle the rum over the top, shake so it mixes through and serve immediately, either plain or with vanilla ice cream.

MENU

WINTER

DINNER   *Serves 4*

Marinated Sardines

**Fillet Steak
with Cucumber & Tomato Sauce**

**Prunes and Oranges in Orange
Sauce**

**Suggested Accompaniments
Plain boiled potatoes** *(20 mins)*
or
Potato & carrot purée *(30 mins – p. 96)*
or
Beans with sesame seeds *(12 min –
p. 88)*

Order of Preparation
1. Place eggs on to hard-boil.

2. Prepare prunes, the orange segments can be added later. Leave prunes cooking gently so they will have time to cook and cool slightly for serving.

3. Prepare marinated sardines completely and leave aside at room temperature. Don't chill them.

4. Make the sauce for the steak and trim the meat.

5. Segment the oranges and mix with the prunes.

Canned sardines are often used in sandwiches or as a quick salad, but they do not have an association with gourmet eating. Marinating the fish however, adds a great deal to its flavour and it is a useful recipe to have on hand for a quick snack at any time.

Fillet steak is the fastest of all meats to cook. This sauce of tomatoes, cucumber and spices is ideal with fillet steak, but could also be used with other cuts of beef or veal scaloppini.

Although the prunes and oranges can be served as soon as they have cooled slightly, the dish improves by longer standing and keeps well for about 4 days in the refrigerator. Buy the really plump dessert prunes for this dish. Or you could use dried apricots. Soak them for 10 minutes and then cook them, covered, in the syrup. They'll take longer to cook than the prunes. Allow about 15 minutes.

MARINATED SARDINES

If you feel that this quantity of sardines is insufficient for 6 people, increase the amount to 500 g (1 lb). The marinade proportions remain the same. But remember that sardines are rich and oily and at their best served in small quantities.

2 eggs	*⅓ cup (2½ fl oz) white vinegar*
400 g (approx. 12 oz) canned sardines	*salt and pepper*
Marinade	*2 teaspoons sugar*
1 small onion, finely diced	*3 tablespoons finely chopped parsley*
¾ cup (6 fl oz) vegetable oil	

Place the eggs in cold water and bring to the boil. Cook until hard-boiled, remove and run cold water over them until they are cool. Place the sardines on a platter which has a raised edge, or into a shallow casserole dish.

Marinade
Put the onion, oil, vinegar, salt, pepper and sugar in a small saucepan and simmer gently for 3 or 4 minutes.

Pour the hot marinade over the sardines and leave them to stand. Although there may appear to be a great deal of liquid, some of this will be absorbed. Leave to marinate for 30 minutes. Remove the sardines, using an egg slice to prevent them from breaking up, and transfer them to a serving platter. Spoon enough of the marinade over the top to moisten them. Peel the eggs and dice them roughly. Scatter on top of the sardines, then sprinkle with parsley. Serve with sliced bread and butter or crusty bread.

Marinated Sardines
Fillet Steak with Cucumber & Tomato Sauce
Prunes & Oranges in Orange Sauce
(see p. 72)

WINTER

Avocado, Bacon & Caviar Appetiser
Split Chicken with Onions
Apple Cream
(see p. 66)

WINTER

FILLET STEAK WITH CUCUMBER AND TOMATO

4 pieces of grilling steak, such as fillet

oil

*4 tablespoons finely chopped
spring onions (scallions)*

Sauce

1 medium-sized cucumber

250 g (8 oz) tomatoes

30 g (1 oz) butter

3 teaspoons Worcestershire sauce

1 clove garlic, crushed

salt and pepper

To make the sauce, place a small saucepan of water on to boil. Peel the cucumber, cut in half and remove the seeds with a teaspoon. Cut the cucumber into small dice and add to the water. Simmer for about 4 minutes.

Place the tomatoes into a small basin and when the cucumber is cooked, strain the liquid over the tomatoes. Leave them for about 10 seconds and then remove from the water and peel the skin away. Cut the tomatoes into small dice.

Melt the butter in a frying pan, add the cucumber and tomato and cook for about 5 minutes or until the tomato has softened. Add the Worcestershire sauce and garlic. Taste for seasoning and set aside; it can be reheated when serving the meat. Trim the steak of any outside fat and flatten slightly. If you are using fillet steak, you need only press down lightly with your hands as it is quite soft.

Place enough oil in a frying pan to moisten the base. Add the steaks when the oil is hot and cook over a high heat until done. They will only take a couple of minutes as the meat has been flattened out. Season with a little salt. Remove and drain. Place a little of the reheated sauce on each plate, scatter the spring onion over this and then place a steak on top.

PRUNES & ORANGES IN ORANGE SYRUP

Instead of brandy I occasionally use brown rum in the syrup.

½ cup (4 fl oz) water

¼ cup (2 oz) caster (powdered) sugar

grated rind of 1 orange

250 g (8 oz) large dessert prunes

½ cup (4 fl oz) orange juice

3 oranges

2 tablespoons brandy

Place the water, sugar and orange rind into a saucepan. Cover and cook gently for 10 minutes. Add the prunes and cook them uncovered over low heat for another 5 minutes. If the liquid starts to boil away, cover the pan. Remove from the heat and place into a bowl. Add the orange juice.

Peel the oranges, being careful to remove all the white bitter pith and then either cut them into thin slices or segment them. Add the oranges to the prunes with the brandy and toss lightly. The prunes can be served warm or chilled with thin cream or sour cream.

WINTER

MENU
DINNER   *Serves 4*

Fish Fillets with Parsley Crumb Coating

Ham Steaks with Mustard Fruit Topping

Liqueur Soufflé Omelette

Order of Preparation
1. Crumb the fish and refrigerate to set the coating.

2. Completely prepare the ham steaks ready for baking.

3. Measure and set out ingredients ready for making the soufflé omelette.

Fish needs a protective coating when fried or sautéed, even if it is just a light coating of flour. Breadcrumbs are a fairly commonplace method of protecting fish, but all sorts of variations can make it more interesting. You can use half crumbs, half finely chopped almonds, you can add herbs to the crumbs (but only a very little as most herbs are too strong for the delicate flavour of the fish), or, as in this recipe you can mix parsley with the crumbs. The parsley gives additional flavour and also an interesting speckled green appearance when it is cooked. Keep the coating light and stand it in the refrigerator for a short time before cooking to set the outside crumbs.

The first time I tried mustard fruit cooked in a dish was at the well-known 'Four Seasons Restaurant' in New York, a popular dining place which epitomises the entire feeling of this city. Sophisticated, a showplace which changes decor to reflect the seasons, they have an appetiser which features prawns wrapped around chopped mustard fruits, then it is cooked in batter and served with a creamy sauce. Since then I have often tried mustard fruits with meat; it gives these ham steaks a spicy flavour and is rather unusual. You can buy the mustard fruits in gourmet shops. They are Italian in origin and the large fruit is suspended in a sweet, spicy syrup. I tried Chinese Chow Chow several times when unable to obtain mustard fruits, it makes an adequate substitute but the flavour is not nearly as good so use these only if the others are impossible to buy. You can prepare the ham steaks in advance. Cover the top of the dish with plastic wrap so it is well sealed, and store for 6 to 8 hours in the refrigerator.

The soufflé omelette can be flavoured with any liqueur. Some of the liqueur is added to the mixture as it cooks, then another spoonful is poured around. I use just a little to flame it with, but you can be as generous as you wish. It is easiest to make it in a non-stick pan. If you use a small pan, 20 cm (8 in) in diameter, the omelette should be turned out flat and broken lightly into four wedges for serving. If made in a huge pan, it won't rise as high but can be folded in half and cut into wedges to serve. Either way it is successful, use a pan you have or buy one which suits other dishes. The omelette must be cooked gently so it sets and browns on the base without burning. It is important to use unsalted butter with a dessert omelette. Serve it with ice cream or with a bowl of fresh fruit.

FISH FILLETS WITH PARSLEY CRUMB COATING

This dish can be prepared with almost any type of fish, provided the fillet has been completely boned and any tough skin removed. Flat fillets of fish such as whiting, John Dory or flounder are best since thick fillets are often undercooked in the centre when the crumb crust is ready.

4 fillets of fish	3 tablespoons finely chopped parsley
salt and pepper	30 g (1 oz) butter
1 egg	¼ cup (2 fl oz) vegetable oil
2 teaspoons oil	lemon wedges for garnish
½ cup (1 oz) crumbs, made from stale bread	

Season the fish with salt and pepper. Beat the egg and oil. Mix the crumbs with the parsley. Dip the fish in the egg and shake gently to remove the excess. Coat with the crumbs, patting and pressing them on to make an even coating. Leave in the refrigerator if you are not cooking the fish immediately.

Place the butter and oil in a frying pan in which the fish will fit in one layer. When very hot, add the fish fillets and cook turning them once, for 3 to 4 minutes or until golden brown on the outside. Fish such as this should be cooked quickly over moderately high heat or the crumbs will become soggy. Drain on kitchen paper and serve immediately with lemon wedges.

HAM STEAKS
WITH MUSTARD FRUIT TOPPING

4 ham steaks

mustard fruits

½ cup (4 fl oz) dry white wine

Sauce

30 g (1 oz) butter

1 tablespoon flour

1 cup (8 fl oz) milk

2 teaspoons dry, English mustard

1 teaspoon French mustard

To make the sauce, melt the butter in a small saucepan and stir in the flour. Cook very gently for a few minutes. Add the milk and stir constantly until it thickens and comes to the boil. Season with the mustards. Don't add salt as the ham will be quite salty enough. Leave the sauce to cook over very low heat for a few minutes while preparing the ham steaks.

Place them in a shallow ovenproof dish. Drain the mustard fruits and chop finely. The quantity you use depends upon the size of the ham steaks. Approximately 1 tablespoon of mustard fruit per steak is generally sufficient. Scatter it lightly in a layer over the top of the steaks. Then spread them with a thin layer of the sauce. Pour the wine around, not over the steaks and set them aside until you are ready to bake them.

Place them in a preheated moderate oven 180°C (350°F/Gas 4) for 12 to 15 minutes or until they're heated through. The longer ham remains in the oven the saltier it becomes, so make sure you don't overcook them.

LIQUEUR SOUFFLÉ OMELETTE

You can partially prepare this in advance, but the egg whites must be beaten and folded in only at the last moment.

3 eggs, separated

2 tablespoons caster (powdered) sugar

2 tablespoons liqueur

30 g (1 oz) unsalted butter

icing (confectioners') sugar

Place the egg yolks in a basin, add the sugar and beat until thick. Add 1 tablespoon of the liqueur and mix.

Melt the butter in the frying pan and pre-heat the griller (broiler).

Beat the egg whites until they hold stiff peaks. Fold them gently into the egg yolk mixture, half at a time. When the butter is foaming, add the omelette and spread it out evenly. Cook over medium heat for 4 to 5 minutes. When the omelette is partly set underneath, place it under the griller and cook for a minute until the top has puffed and it is just firm to touch.

Heat the remaining liqueur, remove the omelette and tilt out onto a plate. Sift the icing sugar over the top. Light the liqueur and pour it around the base of the omelette. Serve immediately, with cream or ice cream.

WINTER

MENU
DINNER *Serves 4*

Chicken in Curry Sauce

Rice Pilaf

Banana Sambal

**Honey & Almond Sauce
with Ice Cream**

Order of Preparation
1. Prepare the chicken curry.

2. Make the rice pilaf; it can be kept warm until ready to serve.

3. Make up the banana sambal.

4. Cook the honey and almond sauce which can be reheated later if necessary.

Curries make some of the best party dishes as they generally improve by being made beforehand and reheated. Because of the time element, this curry has only a rice dish, banana sambal and a bowl of chutney as accompaniments. However you could make it as elaborate as you wish by serving sambals on the table. It is not a particularly hot chicken curry and a commercial curry powder is used as although home-made mixtures are better, they do take considerable time. The spiciness in commercial curry powders varies: there are mild, medium and extra hot mixtures so judge carefully and alter the quantity given to suit your taste. I used a Madras, medium hot curry powder for this recipe and it seems to suit most palates.

The ideal dish after curry is chilled fruit. Unfortunately in winter, there is not a great variety. Occasionally you can find mangoes in the shops which are perfect as a dessert. Chill them and then slice them onto plates. Oranges in Rose Water Sauce (see p. 45) is another excellent choice to follow curry, but if fruit is not used, Honey and Almond Sauce poured over ice cream is a lovely finish to the meal.

CHICKEN IN CURRY SAUCE

---

*1 chicken, weighing about 1.5 kg
(3 lb) cut into portions*

1 tablespoon oil

1 onion

1 clove garlic

1 cooking apple

1 tablespoon curry powder

250 g (8 oz) ripe tomatoes

⅓ cup (2½ fl oz) chicken stock

1 tablespoon mango chutney

¼ teaspoon salt

½ cup (4 fl oz) yoghurt

Heat the oil in a saucepan and add the chicken portions. Sauté them in several batches, rather than overcrowding them in the pan. Cook, turning, until they have changed colour on the outside. As they brown, remove and set aside. While the chicken is browning, dice the onion roughly, chop the garlic, peel, core and slice or dice the apple coarsely. When all the chicken pieces are brown, add the onion, garlic and apple to the pan.

Fry, stirring for a couple of minutes over high heat. Add the curry powder and fry again for a few seconds. Chop the tomatoes roughly, do not skin or seed them as the sauce will be strained later. Place the tomatoes in the pan, cook for a minute or until they have softened slightly, then add the stock, chutney and salt. The amount of salt depends upon the saltiness of the chicken stock, so check first.

Bring the mixture to the boil, place the chicken portions in the pan, cover tightly and simmer very gently for 30 minutes or until the chicken is tender.

Remove the chicken from the saucepan and pour the sauce through a coarse sieve, pressing down on to the vegetables to extract the flavour. If the sauce is too thin, boil rapidly for a couple of minutes and it will thicken. Add the yoghurt, cook until it just lightly coats the back of a spoon and return the chicken to this sauce. Keep warm until serving time.

Note: This dish is most successful made the day before and reheated. Like most curry dishes, it will then acquire even more flavour.

RICE PILAF

2 tablespoons vegetable oil

1½ cups (7½ oz) long grain rice

*2 chicken cubes dissolved in
3 cups (24 fl oz) water,
or 3 cups (24 fl oz) chicken stock*

salt and pepper

30 g (1 oz) butter

Heat the oil in a saucepan and add the rice. Cook over a high heat, stirring with a wooden spoon to ensure it cooks evenly. Continue until much of the rice has become opaque and some of the grains are golden.

Add the water and stock cubes or the chicken stock, salt and pepper. It should bubble and boil almost instantly. Place a lid on the saucepan, turn the heat down to low and cook gently until the rice has absorbed all the liquid and is tender. This takes about 15 minutes. Add the butter and toss with a fork.

If you place the dish at the side of the stove with a towel wrapped around it to retain the heat in the pan, it will still be quite hot, without overcooking, 30 minutes later.

BANANA SAMBAL TO ACCOMPANY CURRY

2 medium-sized bananas

3 teaspoons lemon juice

1 tablespoon finely chopped mint

Peel and slice the bananas into thinnish slices. Place these in a basin and add the lemon juice and mint, mixing well.

It should be eaten when it has been freshly made as the banana softens after about 30 minutes and the dish loses some of its fresh flavour.

HONEY & ALMOND SAUCE

This is a generous quantity for four but any remaining sauce can be kept in a jar for several days and reheated. If kept in the refrigerator it becomes very firm and it is hard to remove from the jar, so leave it at room temperature in a cool place.

45 g (1½ oz) unsalted butter

2 teaspoons cornflour (cornstarch)

¾ cup (6 fl oz) honey

2 tablespoons almond slivers

¼ cup (2 fl oz) fresh orange juice

Melt the butter in a small saucepan and mix with the cornflour. Measure out the honey. (If you pour boiling water into the measuring cup first, the honey will run out easily into the saucepan.) Add the honey, stir over medium heat for about 3 to 4 minutes or until the mixture is beginning to thicken and has large bubbles on top.

Place the almonds in a dry frying pan and cook for a few minutes, tossing the pan until they are golden. Mix into the sauce with the orange juice, cook for 30 seconds and then remove from the stove. It can be left in the saucepan for a short time and reheated, otherwise store in a jar. Serve over ice cream, it is rather sweet and very rich so do not be too generous with it.

EXTRA RECIPES

The recipes in each menu in this book were chosen for their compatibility with each other and because they can be made within an hour. But that doesn't mean that you must stick rigidly to the menus. You can substitute recipes from this section as long as the timing is approximately the same. There may also be times when you do not wish to cook an entire menu but need one fast dish. This section contains a collection of recipes ranging from first courses to desserts which can be either interchanged with the set menus or used as interesting quick additions to any dinner.

FIRST COURSES

CHICKEN LIVERS BETTINA

Serves 4

125 g (4 oz) bacon, cut into small dice

30 g (1 oz) butter

1 onion

125 g (4 oz) mushrooms

1 ripe tomato (about 125 g/4 oz) in weight

250 g (8 oz) chicken livers

salt and pepper

¼ teaspoon mixed dried herbs, or 2 teaspoons fresh chopped herbs

Place the bacon into a saucepan and cook, stirring occasionally until the fat is transparent. Add the butter and allow to melt. While this is cooking, dice the onion and add. Leave to cook gently for a few minutes.

Cut the stalks of the mushrooms level with the caps and slice thinly. Add these to the pan. Pour boiling water over the tomato in either a small basin or cup and leave to stand for ten seconds. Pour away the water and skin the tomato. Chop the tomato in small dice and add with the chicken livers, salt, pepper and herbs.

Fry, stirring for about 5 minutes or until the liver has changed colour and the sauce is thick. Stir the mixture occasionally, but do not break up the livers. Check for seasoning before serving. It can be kept warm without spoiling for a short time, but do not cook the livers for too long, as they are best with just the barest tinge of pink in the centre.

EGGS BAKED IN TOMATO CASES

Although the eggs in this recipe are baked in the tomatoes, there is a tendency for them to overflow as they begin to cook. Thus they are much easier to prepare and serve if the tomatoes are actually cooked in individual dishes or casseroles. A small soufflé dish for example, will hold a tomato perfectly.

Serves 4

4 ripe tomatoes, weighing approximately 125-150 g (4-5 oz) each

salt and pepper

pinch sugar

a little fresh or dried basil

4 small eggs

4 teaspoons thick cream

4 thin slices Gruyère, the size of the top of the tomatoes

Place the tomatoes on a board to check if they will balance. If not, cut a tiny piece from the base to make them stable. Cut the top away, then using a teaspoon, remove most of the flesh and all of the seeds from the inside. Season the tomato with salt, pepper and sugar. Chop a little fresh basil and add a sprinkle to each one or place a pinch of dried basil in each tomato. Place the tomatoes in the containers ready to bake.

Break the eggs, one at a time, into a cup and gently pour them into the tomatoes. Season the top of the eggs, and place a teaspoon of cream on each one. Put the slice of Gruyère cheese on top to completely cover the egg. Stand the tomatoes in their little casseroles on a flat baking tray for easy handling. Cook in a moderate oven, 180°C (350°F/Gas 4) for about 20 minutes or until the egg has just set. Be careful not to overcook the egg (the cheese on top will puff up slightly when the egg is ready). Remove from the oven and leave them to settle for a minute before serving with strips of hot buttered toast.

SPINACH & CHEESE QUICHE WITHOUT A CRUST

As this quiche is served directly from the oven to the table and cannot be turned out, it is best served in a china quiche dish. In its absence, a pie dish or shallow round ovenproof dish is suitable. The dish should be 20 cm (8 in) to 23 cm (9 in) in diameter.

Serves 4

250 g (8 oz) packet frozen spinach

100 g (3 oz) bacon, rind removed

30 g (1 oz) butter

1 medium-sized onion, finely diced

4 eggs, beaten

1 cup (8 fl oz) thick cream

2 tablespoons grated Parmesan cheese

60 g (2 oz) Gruyère, or a Swiss melting cheese

salt and pepper

1 large ripe tomato

Place the block of frozen spinach into a saucepan, cover and cook until soft, stirring occasionally to break up the icy bits. Drain and leave in a sieve. While the spinach is cooking, cut the bacon into small dice or long strips and place in a dry frying pan. Cook over a high heat, stirring for a few minutes to cook it evenly. When it is crisp, remove from the pan and drain off the fat. Add the butter to the same pan and sauté the onion until slightly softened, but do not let it brown. Return the bacon to the pan with the spinach, eggs, cream and Parmesan. Cut the Gruyère cheese into small dice and add it to the pan. Add a little salt and pepper (not too much as the cheeses, particularly the Parmesan, can be salty). Mix together well with a fork and pour into the buttered quiche dish. Slice the tomato thinly and arrange the slices over the top. Season the tomato, which will not sink as the filling is quite thick. Place in a moderate oven, 180°C (350°F/Gas 4) and bake for about 25 minutes or until the filling has set. Leave to stand for 5 minutes before slicing into wedges. It can be served piping hot but is also good when only barely warm.

SALAD OF ENDIVE WITH CRESS & ORANGE

This has one of the most confusing names of all vegetables. It is sometimes called chicory and at other times witloof, a name given by the Belgians who actually developed the vegetable. It does not really matter what you call it as long as you use the correct vegetable for this salad. Its tightly packed leaves are yellow-white in colour with a fresh, slightly bitter flavour. Green tips on the vegetable means additional bitterness so buy Belgian endive as pale in colour as possible.

Serves 4

2 Belgian endive

½ bunch watercress

2 medium-sized oranges

2 teaspoons sugar

3 tablespoons vegetable or olive oil

1 tablespoon white vinegar

2 tablespoons orange juice

Dressing

1 tablespoon French mustard

1 teaspoon hot English mustard

Cut the base from the endive and then cut away the top leafy part. Cut the stalks into several long strips and place these instantly into water in which there are a few ice cubes.

Wash the watercress well, break off the tips only and discard the stalky or tough parts. Drain the watercress on kitchen paper. Peel the oranges, cut into thin slices or segments and chill them until you are ready to assemble the salad.

Dressing

Mix all the ingredients together, whisking with a fork, so that it is thick.

Place the endive strips around the edge of a platter and heap the watercress tips in the centre. Spoon the dressing over both and then arrange the oranges on top of the watercress. Once you pour the dressing over, serve within about 10 minutes.

RICE & PASTA

RICE WITH PRAWNS

Although it is preferable to use green prawns for this dish, as the shells make a light stock for the rice, if they are unavailable cooked prawns could also be used. When using them, follow the recipe in the same manner, using the cooked shells to make some stock.

Serves 4

500 g (1 lb) raw prawns

5 cups (1.25 litres) water

½ teaspoon salt

1 onion

2 tablespoons oil

2 cups (10 oz) long grain rice

1 tablespoon tomato paste

stock from the prawn shells

3 tablespoons finely grated Parmesan cheese

45 g (1½ oz) butter

Shell the prawns and place the shells in a saucepan with the water and salt. Bring to the boil, cover and cook over low heat 10 to 15 minutes.

Dice the onion and place in a heavy-based saucepan with the oil. Fry for a few minutes, stirring until slightly softened. Add the rice to the saucepan and fry until the grains have become golden and opaque. It is essential to keep stirring all the time or it will colour unevenly and catch on the base.

Strain the prawn stock into a basin, measure out four cups (1 litre) and mix the tomato paste with this. Pour the stock over the rice, which will bubble and boil almost instantly. Cover, reduce the heat and cook for about 10 minutes or until partly tender.

While this is cooking, chop the prawns into small pieces. With a fork make a little hollow in the centre of the rice, place the prawn pieces in this and then push some rice over the top of them. They will steam in this hollow.

Replace the lid on the pan and continue cooking until the rice is tender. It should only take another 5 minutes. When ready to serve, add the grated cheese and the butter, cut into small pieces. Using two forks, turn gently to mix and to distribute the prawns throughout the mixture.

RICE WITH SULTANAS & ALMONDS

Serves 6

2 tablespoons oil

1 white onion, finely chopped

1½ cups (8 oz) long grain rice

3 cups (24 fl oz) chicken stock or water

1 piece cinnamon stick, about the size of a finger

4 tablespoons sultanas (seedless raisins)

salt and pepper

60 g (2 oz) almond slivers

45 g (1½ oz) butter

Heat the oil and add the onion, cook for a few minutes, stirring occasionally until the onion has softened slightly. Add the rice and turn up the heat, fry rapidly until the rice grains have become opaque and some are slightly tinged with gold. You must stir continuously or the rice will burn.

Add the chicken stock, push the cinnamon stick into the centre of the rice and add the sultanas. Immediately the liquid comes to the boil cover with a tight-fitting lid. Leave to cook over low heat for approximately 15 minutes or until the rice grains are tender and have absorbed all the liquid. Taste to check, they should be firm but not hard in the centre. If the rice becomes dry as it cooks, add a few more spoonfuls of liquid.

While this is cooking, place the almond slivers into a frying pan and toss them in the dry pan over a medium heat until they are slightly toasted and golden in colour. Mix the almonds into the rice. Then cut the butter into three pieces, mix into the rice and fluff with two forks. As this is done the butter will melt and the almonds will become evenly distributed throughout. Remove the cinnamon stick before serving.

If you are not ready to serve the rice instantly, it does not spoil if kept aside. It retains heat for some time and if correctly cooked may soften a little more but will never become sticky.

Alternatively, you can brown the rice, add the stock, sultanas and liquid, cover and then remove from the heat. When needed, bring the liquid to the boil and cook the rice, decreasing the cooking time by a few minutes.

LUCIANO'S MIDNIGHT PASTA

Lake Como is one of the loveliest diadems of Italy's lakes district, its villas and towns steeped in history and legend. On the shores of Como, near the tiny village of Cernobbio, is the Villa d'Este, one of the luxury hotels in the area. Its history dates back to the sixteenth century and one of the most famous owners, the tragic Caroline of Brunswick, much-maligned would-be Queen of England, spent a great deal of her time and fortune restoring and redecorating the Villa.

Despite an international guest list, the cooking remains distinctly Italian. The young and very good looking chef at the Villa, Luciano Pariolari, cooks pasta for meals at the hotel but says that midnight is about the only time that a true Italian would eat pasta as the main dish. At other times it is only served as a first course. This pasta dish is spicy and should be served directly from the pan at the table. The chilli can be adjusted according to individual tastes. A considerable amount of olive oil is used and as many of the oils sold outside Italy are heavier than their fresh young oils, I find it more successful to use only half olive, half vegetable oil which lightens the flavour.

Serves 4

375 g (12 oz) fine spaghetti

1 tablespoon salt

1 tablespoon oil

Sauce

½ cup (4 fl oz) olive oil

1 small fresh chilli

2 large garlic cloves, crushed

3 tablespoons finely chopped parsley

3 tablespoons freshly grated Parmesan cheese

Bring a large pan of water to the boil, adding salt and oil. Place in the spaghetti and as it softens, push it down into the water. Stir and leave to cook over a high heat until it is tender. Judge by testing a strand, it should be just firm to the teeth. Drain well.

Sauce

Warm the oil gently in a pan. Cut the chilli in half and wash out the seeds. Chop up and measure about 1 tablespoon; more or even less of the chilli can be used as they can vary in degrees of heat. Add the chilli to the oil with the garlic and leave the mixture to warm but do not fry or the garlic will brown and become bitter.

Add the drained pasta and turn over in the oil to coat. Mix in the parsley and cheese and serve immediately with an additional bowl of Parmesan cheese on the table.

SPAGHETTI WITH PINE NUTS, TOMATO & ANCHOVY SAUCE

Serves 4

375 g (12 oz) spaghetti

1 tablespoon salt

1 tablespoon oil

Sauce

90 g (3 oz) butter

1 white onion, finely diced

500 g (1 lb) ripe tomatoes

50 g (1¾ oz) pine nuts

pepper

½ teaspoon sugar

45 g (1½ oz) flat anchovy fillets, chopped

3 tablespoons finely chopped parsley

Spaghetti

Bring a large pan of water to the boil and add the salt and oil. Add the spaghetti gradually so the water remains boiling and cook the spaghetti until it is barely tender. The way to judge is by taste: it should be just firm when you bite a strand.

Drain and leave aside. It can be used immediately or reheated in the sauce.

Sauce

Melt 30 g of the butter in a frying pan and add the onion. Sauté, stirring occasionally until slightly softened. Remove the skin of the tomatoes by either pouring boiling water over them, or if the spaghetti is cooking, dropping the tomatoes into the water for a few seconds. Remove them with a slotted spoon. This saves boiling up water separately.

Peel the tomatoes and cut into quite small pieces, but do not seed them. Add the pine nuts to the onion when it has softened, stir for a minute or until the pine nuts have become slightly golden, then add the tomatoes. Increase the heat and cook the tomatoes, seasoning with pepper and sugar until they have softened. The sauce should taste very fresh so the tomatoes only need about 3 minutes cooking. Add the anchovies. You can prepare the sauce up to this stage beforehand and reheat.

When ready to serve with the spaghetti, add the parsley to the hot sauce, mix in the remaining butter cut into a couple of pieces and stir only until it melts. The sauce should be creamy. Place it in a large bowl or in the pan in which you cooked the spaghetti. Add the spaghetti and turn to mix them together, tasting for seasoning. Now is the time to add salt; this is done only at the end as it depends on the saltiness of the anchovies. Serve a bowl of Parmesan cheese on the table separately.

VEGETABLES

BEAN SHOOTS WITH GINGER

Serves 4

1 tablespoon vegetable oil

1 onion, roughly chopped

1 clove garlic, crushed

1 teaspoon grated fresh ginger

250 g (8 oz) bean shoots

salt

¼ teaspoon sugar

2 tablespoons soy sauce

Heat the oil in a frying pan and add the onion. Fry for a couple of minutes over medium heat, stirring constantly, until the onion has slightly softened. Add the garlic and the ginger and cook for 30 seconds, then add the bean shoots and season with salt and sugar. Toss them during the couple of minutes it takes to cook them. Add the soy sauce, mix through and serve.

Be cautious with the salt as the saltiness of soy sauce varies. Taste first by placing a little on the tip of your tongue. If very salty only use the tiniest bit of salt in this dish and then season again at the finish if necessary.

BEANS WITH SESAME SEEDS

Serves 4

500 g (1 lb) stringless beans

salt

2 tablespoons sesame seeds

45 g (1½ oz) butter

Place a pot of water on to boil. Top and tail the beans and place them, a third at a time, into the water, keeping the heat high. When it is boiling again, season with salt. Cook over rapid heat, uncovered for about 10 minutes or until the beans are just tender.

While they are cooking, place the sesame seeds in a dry frying pan and cook over medium heat, tossing occasionally until they are golden and toasted. Set aside.

Drain the beans, add the sesame seeds and the butter and shake or stir until they are coated with the seeds. They adhere very easily to the outside of the beans.

BEANS WITH KAISER FLEISCH

Kaiser Fleisch is a continental smoked bacon and has a wonderful affinity with beans. It can be bought in delicatessens in small chunky pieces. If you cannot obtain this, use the equivalent amount of bacon in this recipe.

Serves 4	*2 teaspoons lemon juice*
500 g (1 lb) stringless beans	*salt and pepper*
125 g (4 oz) Kaiser Fleisch	
30 g (1 oz) butter	

Place a large pot of water on to boil. Top and tail the beans, often it is easiest to do this with your fingers rather than a knife. When the water is boiling, add the beans, about a third at a time. Salt the water only when all the beans are added. Boil rapidly for about 10 minutes or until they are just tender.

While the beans are cooking, trim away the rind from the Kaiser Fleisch and then cut it into thin strips with a small sharp knife. Place the Kaiser Fleisch in a small saucepan and cook, stirring occasionally, until it is crisp. Set aside.

Drain the beans and mix in the Kaiser Fleisch and any fat around it. Add the butter, season with salt and pepper and stir the mixture. Serve immediately.

BROCCOLI WITH ALMONDS & PIMENTO

Broccoli is a little like asparagus to cook in that if you are not careful, the flower heads soften and break before the stalks are tender. Choose broccoli that have tight green tops. If there are yellow flowers, the broccoli is old and will be strong in flavour.

Serves 4	*60 g (2 oz) almond slivers*
500 g (1 lb) broccoli	*220 g (7 oz) canned pimentoes*
60 g (2 oz) butter	*salt and pepper*

Pull away the leaves from the broccoli and cut off the closed flower ends, leaving just a short piece of stalk. If the stalks are hard and tough-looking, peel them with a knife or vegetable peeler. Bring a large pot of water to the boil and add salt. Add the broccoli heads and cook, uncovered, until they are just tender.

While they are cooking melt 30 g of the butter, add the almonds and cook for a minute or two until golden. Shake the pan occasionally so they will colour evenly. Drain the pimento, dice very small, and mix with the almonds.

Drain the broccoli well and place on a heated platter. Season. Add the remaining butter to the pan with the almonds and pimento, leave a few seconds to just barely melt and then pour this mixture over the top of the broccoli. Broccoli seems to become cold very quickly so needs to be served as soon as it is ready.

SLICED CAULIFLOWER WITH PINE NUTS

Serves 4

45 g (1½ oz) butter

30 g (1 oz) pine nuts

1 medium-sized onion, roughly chopped

500 g (1 lb) cauliflower

salt and pepper

1 cup (8 fl oz) water or chicken stock

Melt the butter in a frying pan and add the pine nuts and onion. Cook these together for a few minutes over medium heat while preparing the cauliflower. If the pine nuts show signs of becoming too brown, remove from the heat.

Cut the cauliflower into quarters and then, placing the flat side down on a board, cut into slices. Start at the coarse stalky end and cut very thinly; when you reach the flowerets you can cut thicker strips. Add the cauliflower to the pine nuts in the pan and cook for about 6 minutes. Keep the heat high and toss with a spoon or spatula occasionally. Sprinkle the top generously with salt and pepper as it is cooking. Add the water or stock and boil this away completely. By the time the liquid has gone, the cauliflower should be tender.

The dish will have just a slight bite to the teeth and although it will not be white in colour, more a cream or light brown, it has a delicious nutty flavour.

CAULIFLOWER WITH CHEESE & CREAM SAUCE

This quantity of cauliflower should be sufficient for four because it is quite rich. However if you wish you can use 500 g (1 lb) cauliflower and cook in a slightly wider frying pan with the same amount of butter, oil and water. You can use a little extra cheese and cream, although the specified quantity will still give the cauliflower plenty of flavour.

Serves 4

375 g (12 oz) cauliflower

30 g (1 oz) butter

3 teaspoons oil

salt and pepper

¾ cup (6 fl oz) water

½ cup (4 fl oz) thick cream

¾ cup (3 oz) grated Gruyère cheese or a Swiss melting cheese

Cut the cauliflower into quarters. Then, placing the flat side down, cut across into slices. Start at the stalky ends and cut thinly, when you come to the flowerets, leave them in thicker strips.

Melt the butter and heat the oil in a frying pan. Add the cauliflower to the pan and toss over high heat for a few minutes until it turns pale golden. Season with salt and pepper, add the water and cook over high heat until the water has completely cooked away and the cauliflower is just tender. It will have a slightly crunchy texture when cooked this way but if too firm, just add a little extra water and continue cooking. The cauliflower can be left in the pan and reheated but add the cheese and cream only at the last moment.

Blend the cream and cheese together. Pour over the cauliflower and mix. The cheese will melt and form a sauce. Once it is hot, remove from the heat, if you continue to cook it, it will become stringy.

Vegetables

Mushroom Salad with Walnut Dressing
Chicken on a Bed of Peas & Ham
Pears in Passionfruit Sauce
(see p. 60)

AutumN

Eggs New Orleans Style
Orange Gratin
(see p. 62)

WINTER

SAUTÉED CARROTS & ONIONS

Serves 4

375 g (12 oz) whole baby carrots	30 g (1 oz) butter
salt	1 tablespoon oil
1 onion	1 teaspoon sugar
	pepper

Wash the carrots well or peel them if necessary. Place them in salted water and cook until just tender. While they are cooking, cut the onion in half and then into thin slices. Heat the butter and oil in a saucepan, add the onion slices and sauté, stirring occasionally until slightly softened.

Drain the carrots well, add them to the onion with the sugar and cook for another 5 minutes or until the onion has become very soft and the carrots glazed. Season with pepper and serve.

SHREDDED CABBAGE WITH BACON

Serves 4

375 g (12 oz) cabbage	30 g (1 oz) butter
125 g (4 oz) bacon	½ teaspoon sugar
	salt and pepper

Discard any tough outer leaves and the stalk and cut the cabbage into shreds, not too finely. Wash the cabbage shreds and place in a saucepan with enough water to cover the base of the pan. Season with salt, cover the pan and cook the cabbage for about 12 minutes or until just tender.

Cut the bacon into long thin strips and while the cabbage is cooking, fry this in a dry frying pan until the fat is transparent and the bacon cooked. Set aside. Do not drain, as the fat is used with the cabbage to add additional flavour.

Drain the cabbage well. Place the butter in the saucepan, add the sugar, cabbage and bacon with any fat and toss for a moment until it is hot. Season, being cautious with the salt until you taste the dish as the bacon will add considerable saltiness.

EGGPLANT CHIPS

Although good as an accompaniment to meats, these chips of eggplant can also be nibbled with drinks as an appetizer. Choose carefully when you buy, as the eggplants should be shiny and firm. Reject any which are wrinkled or dull as these will often have a bitter taste when cooked.

Serves 4

500 g (1 lb) eggplant (aubergine)	1 cup (8 fl oz) milk
salt and pepper	½ cup (2 oz) flour
	vegetable oil

Peel the eggplant, cut into long strips, exactly as you would for making rather large chips. You can leave the skin on if the eggplants are fresh, otherwise the skin can taste strong and bitter.

Place the eggplant on a board and scatter some salt over the top. Leave to stand for about 15 minutes. Wash lightly in a sieve and then drain on kitchen paper. Put the eggplant in a basin and cover with the milk. Stand for about 5 minutes and then strain. Place the flour in a paper bag, add the eggplant strips and holding the end of the bag firmly, shake to coat them with flour. Turn them directly into a strainer or sieve so the excess flour will fall away.

Use either a saucepan of heated oil or a deep fryer. The oil should be heated to the point that one chip sizzles instantly when tested. Cook the eggplant chips, half at a time, until they are crisp and golden. Drain on kitchen paper and season generously with salt and pepper. Serve instantly as they become soft if kept longer than 5 minutes.

VEGETABLES

SAUTÉED LETTUCE & ONIONS

Serves 4

30 g (1 oz) butter

2 medium-sized onions

1 lettuce, weighing about 500 g (1 lb)

½ cup (4 fl oz) chicken stock

salt and pepper

Melt the butter gently in a frying pan. Peel the onions, cut in half, place the cut side down on a board, and cut into thin slices. Sauté the onion gently in the butter until it has barely started to soften.

While this is cooking, shred the lettuce thinly, removing any very tough centre stalks. Add the lettuce to the pan and cook for a few minutes until it becomes limp. Then add the stock, salt and pepper and cook again until the lettuce is tender. Do not let it overcook, it should still have a slightly firm texture. If there is too much liquid around the lettuce, turn up the heat and cook some away.

ONIONS COOKED IN WHITE WINE

Serves 4

4 large onions

45 g (1½ oz) butter

1 teaspoon sugar

salt and pepper

½ cup (4 fl oz) dry white wine

Peel the onions, cut in half and then cut across to make about 8 wedges, rather like an apple. Place these wedges in a small saucepan with the butter and cook for a couple of minutes, stirring until they are coated with butter. Add the sugar, salt and pepper and continue cooking until the onions are tinged with golden edges. Keep the heat fairly high under them, but be careful not to burn them. Add the white wine, turn the heat down and continue cooking until the onions have completely softened and the wine has almost evaporated. If the onions are not becoming soft you can place a lid on the pan for about 5 minutes.

Altogether the onions should take approximately 20 minutes to cook. These can be cooked in advance and reheated.

BAKED POTATO SLICES

Serves 4

500 g (1 lb) old potatoes

30 g (1 oz) butter

1 tablespoon oil

salt and pepper

Wash the potatoes but do not peel them. Cut into thick slices.

Warm the butter and oil in a small saucepan until the butter has melted. Use a tray to cook the potato slices, such as a Swiss roll (jelly roll) tin in preference to a china dish. Brush the base of the tin with a little of the butter and oil. Place the potato slices on top in a single layer and then trickle the remainder of the butter and oil over the top.

Season generously with salt and pepper and place in a moderate oven, 180°C (350°F/Gas 4) for about 30 minutes or until tender. At the end of this time they will be cooked but if you prefer a crisper potato slice, cook for another 15 to 20 minutes and a golden crust will form.

VEGETABLES

CREAM COOKED POTATOES

This is best done with small potatoes which can just be cut in half, but if these are unavailable, cut larger potatoes into even-sized portions or big chunky pieces. Use new potatoes, old potatoes will break up in the cream.

Serves 4

500 g (1 lb) potatoes

½ cup (4 fl oz) sour cream

salt and pepper

1 tablespoon finely chopped chives

Peel the potatoes, cut each into half or chunky pieces and place them in a saucepan. Add enough cold water just to cover, and salt the water. Bring to the boil and cook gently for about 10 minutes or until partly tender. Drain. Return the potatoes to the saucepan, pour the sour cream over the top, add a little salt and pepper. Cover the saucepan and cook over a gentle heat for a further 10 minutes or until the potatoes are quite soft. Check after 7 minutes to see that the cream sauce has not evaporated. Do not be concerned if the cream looks very oily as it cooks. When ready, shake or stir to mix the potatoes with the liquid in the pan, scatter the chives on top and serve.

POTATO CUBES WITH GARLIC & PARSLEY

You can make this with either new or old potatoes but new potatoes take a little longer to cook.

Serves 4

750 g (1½ lb) potatoes

1 tablespoon vegetable oil

30 g (1 oz) butter

salt and pepper

3 tablespoons finely chopped parsley

2 cloves garlic, crushed

Peel the potatoes and cut into dice about the size of a small walnut. Heat the oil and butter in a heavy-based frying pan and when foaming add the potatoes, seasoning with salt and pepper. Stir to coat them with the oil.

Cook them for about 20 minutes, stirring occasionally and if they are not cooking through you can place a lid on the pan for a few minutes, which will soften them. They should be quite tender on the inside and brown and crisp on the outside.

Mix the parsley and garlic together. Just before serving, scatter the parsley and garlic over the top and stir to mix.

POTATO & CARROT PURÉE

Serves 4

500 g (1 lb) potatoes

250 g (8 oz) carrots

salt

30 g (1 oz) butter

2 tablespoons cream

pepper and additional salt if needed

2 tablespoons finely chopped chives
for garnish

Peel the potatoes and if large cut into several big pieces; if small, leave them whole. Peel the carrots and cut them into chunky pieces. Place both the potatoes and carrots into a saucepan, cover with cold water and add some salt. Bring to the boil, cover and simmer gently for about 20 to 25 minutes or until they are both cooked. Drain.

Either mash well or place into a food processor and process until smooth. Return them to the saucepan, add the butter, cream and seasoning and warm through, stirring rapidly with a wooden spoon. Serve in a mound on a plate, scattering the chives over the top.

POTATOES LYONNAISE

Serves 4

750 g (1½ lb) small potatoes

salt

30 g (1 oz) butter

2 tablespoons vegetable oil

2 onions

salt and pepper

Peel the potatoes and cut them in half if small, and into quarters if large. Place in a saucepan, cover with cold water and season with salt. Bring to the boil, cover and cook gently until tender. Do not allow them to become too soft. Drain well.

Peel and cut the onions in half while the potatoes are cooking. Place them flat-side down on a board and cut into thinnish slices. Heat the butter and oil in a heavy-based frying pan, add the onions and cook for a few minutes, stirring occasionally until they are limp. Add the drained potatoes to the pan and continue cooking until the onion is soft and pale gold and the potatoes are slightly coloured.

The secret of this potato dish is to adjust the heat so that the onions and potatoes cook at the same time, the onions becoming soft but not dark in colour, and the potatoes cooking quickly enough so that they do not become soggy. Season with additional salt and a little pepper.

Note: The potatoes can be cooked beforehand, then reheated in the pan with the butter, oil and onions.

VEGETABLES

POTATOES WITH PAPRIKA AND CAPSICUM SAUCE

Serves 4

750 g (1½ lb) small potatoes, peeled

1 large red or green capsicum (bell pepper)

30 g (1 oz) butter

1 tablespoon vegetable oil

1 tablespoon paprika

½ cup (4 fl oz) sour cream

salt and pepper

Wash the potatoes and cut in half. Place them in a saucepan, cover with cold water and season with salt. Bring to the boil, cover and cook until they are just tender.

While they are cooking, cut the capsicum in half, removing the seeds. Cut into thin strips. Heat the butter and oil in a frying pan and add the capsicum. Leave to sauté gently, giving it an occasional stir until it has softened. Add the paprika and stir to mix, then add the sour cream and warm through.

Drain the potatoes well and place them in the frying pan. Mix gently with the sour cream sauce until they are coated. Season with salt and pepper if necessary.

Note: The potatoes can be cooked beforehand, then warmed again in the sauce.

SAUTÉED POTATO CUBES

This dish can be made with either new or old potatoes but new potatoes take a little longer to cook.

It is a most successful accompaniment to many meat or chicken dishes and as long as you remember to stir the potatoes occasionally, it cooks away gently on its own.

Serves 4

750 g (1½ lb) potatoes

1 tablespoon vegetable oil

30 g (1 oz) butter

salt and pepper

Peel the potatoes and cut them into dice. The larger the dice, the longer the potatoes will take to cook; they should be slightly smaller than a walnut.

Heat the oil and butter in a heavy-based frying pan. When foaming, add the potatoes, season with salt and pepper and stir to coat. Leave them to cook for about 20 minutes, giving an occasional stir. If they are not cooking through you can rest a lid on top of the pan. When ready they should be crisp and brown on the outside and tender on the inside.

VEGETABLES

SNOW PEAS

This amount of peas (250 g) should be sufficient as an accompaniment as there will be no wastage. Buy peas only just barely protruding through the shell, as over-developed peas will be tougher. Always expensive to buy, they have a wonderful delicate taste but must be cooked until only just tender, never allowed to become limp and dull in colour.

Serves 4

250 g (8 oz) snow peas (mange tout)

½ teaspoon salt

1 teaspoon sugar

Top and tail the snow pea pods, pulling away the string as you do this. It is quicker to do this with your fingers than with a knife. Bring a pan of water to the boil while you are preparing the peas. Season with the salt and sugar and add the snow peas. Keep the water on a rapid boil and cook for only about 3 minutes. Drain them and serve immediately. You can toss them with a spoonful of light vegetable oil before serving or mix a little butter through and leave it to melt, but this last step is optional.

BABY SQUASH WITH BUTTER AND ROSEMARY

These little squash are also known as Custard Marrow. A very attractive little vegetable with a delicate pale green colour and tiny scalloped edge, the smallest ones are the nicest to eat. Try to buy them when only 4 cm (1½ in) across or even smaller.

Serves 4

375 g (12 oz) squash

30 g (1 oz) butter

2 teaspoons finely chopped rosemary (see Note)

salt and pepper

Trim away the little stalks on top of the squash and place them in a saucepan. Cover with cold water, season with salt and cook, covered, for 12 to 15 minutes or until tender. Drain them.

Place the butter in the same saucepan, adding the rosemary and when the butter has melted, return the squash to the pan. Toss for a moment and season with salt and pepper.

Note: I always use fresh rosemary for this dish but a pinch of dried rosemary, while not as good, could be substituted. Cut the fresh rosemary in very tiny pieces or it can taste unpleasantly stalky in dishes.

VEGETABLES

GARLIC-SCENTED TOMATOES

In this simple dish of baked tomatoes, garlic slivers are placed in the flesh of the tomato and removed before serving. It gives them a very delicate garlic flavour and sweetness.

Serves 4	*sugar*
4 ripe tomatoes	*butter*
salt and pepper	*2 cloves garlic*

Cut the tomatoes in half and season the top of each one with salt and pepper and a tiny pinch of sugar. Peel the garlic and cut into thick slivers. Insert a couple of these into the top of each tomato half.

Place the tomatoes in a shallow ovenproof dish. Put the tiniest piece of butter (about the size of a pea) on top of each one and bake them in a moderate oven, 180°C (350°F/Gas 4) for 12 to 15 minutes or until just tender. Before serving, remove the garlic pieces.

SAUTÉED ZUCCHINI

Serves 4	*45 g (1½ oz) butter*
8 small zucchini (courgettes)	*1 tablespoon peanut or light vegetable oil*
salt and pepper	*1 tablespoon water*

Cut the ends from the zucchini. Cut them in half lengthwise and season the outside with salt and pepper. Place the butter and oil in a frying pan. Add the zucchini, cut-side down. Cook over medium heat until golden, turn and cook the other side. Add the water, turn the heat up and cook the water away.

The dish should take approximately 12 minutes to cook and should still have a slightly crisp texture.

VEGETABLES

SAUTÉED ZUCCHINI WITH TOMATO

Choose small, thin zucchini for this dish. Zucchini weighing between 100-125 g (3½-4 oz) each are the perfect weight.

Serves 4

4 zucchini (courgettes)

45 g (1½ oz) butter

3 teaspoons vegetable oil

1 tablespoon tomato paste

½ cup (4 fl oz) water

¼ teaspoon salt

black pepper

1 large clove garlic

Place the butter and oil in a large frying pan to heat while preparing the zucchini. Wash the zucchini, remove the tops and cut them in half lengthwise. Place them, cut side down, in the butter. Cook over a medium heat so the butter will not brown, turning once, for about 10 minutes or until they have softened slightly.

Mix together in a small basin, the tomato paste, water, salt and pepper. Leave the skin on the garlic, cut in half and place in the liquid. Pour this mixture over the zucchini and continue cooking until it has reduced away to just a glaze in the pan. Turn once or twice, so the zucchini are evenly coated with the tomato. The zucchini should be tender. If not, place a lid over the top for a few minutes to soften them. It's not important for the lid to fit on top, you can rest it on the vegetables and it will retain some steam. Remove the garlic and serve.

CRISPY ZUCCHINI STRIPS

These little crunchy strips of zucchini are so good that they can be nibbled as a savoury with drinks. It is essential to make them at the last moment, although the zucchini can be cut and coated with the flour an hour or so beforehand without spoiling.

Serves 4

500 g (1 lb) zucchini (courgettes)

½ cup (2 oz) flour

salt and pepper

oil for frying

3 tablespoons finely grated Parmesan cheese

Remove the ends from the zucchini. Cut in half horizontally and then cut the zucchini into long, thick strips lengthwise, rather like large chips. Season the flour with salt and pepper, place in a paper bag and add the zucchini. Shake until coated. Pour the contents of the bag into a sieve or colander and shake; the excess flour will fall through.

Heat the oil until a piece of zucchini dropped into it sizzles instantly. Add the zucchini, half at a time, and fry for about 5 minutes or until crispy on the outside and tender inside. Remove to kitchen paper to drain and season lightly with salt and pepper. Cook the second batch, then scatter Parmesan cheese lightly over the top of the strips when serving.

If the first batch has cooled, return them to the hot oil for thirty seconds and it will reheat the strips and crisp them again.

VEGETABLES

SAUTÉED GRATED ZUCCHINI

This dish can be very quickly prepared using a food processor.

Serves 4

500 g (1 lb) zucchini (courgettes)

salt

45 g (1½ oz) butter

pepper

Top and tail the zucchini and grate them. Place in a basin in several layers, scattering salt over the layers and leave to stand for 20 to 30 minutes. Remove the zucchini and squeeze in your hands, straining through a sieve is not sufficient.

Melt the butter in a frying pan and add the grated zucchini, tossing over high heat for about 3 to 4 minutes or until tender. Season with pepper, but it is not necessary to add any more salt.

This dish can be prepared beforehand, but is nicer if cooked just before serving time.

BAKED PUMPKIN CUBES
WITH SESAME SEEDS

While any dry, baking pumpkin is suitable, butternut pumpkins are exceptionally good when prepared this way.

Serves 4

1 kg (2 lb) pumpkin

1 tablespoon vegetable oil

30 g (1 oz) butter

salt and pepper

2 tablespoons sesame seeds

Peel the pumpkin, remove any seeds and then cut into cubes. They should be about the size of a walnut. You can make them larger, but the cooking time will be extended slightly. Place the pumpkin in a shallow ovenproof dish. Trickle the oil over the top. Cut the butter into a few pieces and place these on top, then season the pumpkin with salt and pepper. Cook in a moderate oven, 180°C (350°F/Gas 4) for about 15 minutes. Occasionally stir the pumpkin cubes with a fork or spoon, moving the pumpkin on the base to the top. Scatter the sesame seeds over the pumpkin and cook for another 10 to 15 minutes or until the pumpkin is tender.

FISH

FISH IN MANGO SAUCE

I find that fillets of whiting are the nicest of all in this dish. If they are unobtainable, other fish fillets can be used, as long as they are fine-textured.

Serves 4	**Sauce**
8 fillets of whiting, weighing approximately 60 g (2 oz) each	*1 cup (8 fl oz) dry white wine*
	½ cup (4 fl oz) thick cream
flour	*1 mango*
salt and pepper	*salt and pepper*
45 g (1½ oz) butter	

Remove any little pieces of fin which are left on the whiting (even though it is filleted this often remains). Dip in the flour which has been seasoned with salt and pepper. Shake away any excess.

Heat the butter in a large frying pan and when hot add the whiting. Cook, turning once until cooked through: a very thin fish, whiting cooks quickly and takes only a couple of minutes. Remove to a heated platter, cover and keep warm.

Sauce

To make the sauce, use the same pan in which the fish was cooked. Wipe out with some kitchen paper. Pour in the wine and cream and keep the heat high to reduce. While it is reducing, peel the mango and cut into slices. It is best to peel half first, remove the slices, turn it over and then peel the other half and slice. Otherwise the mango slides and is very wet to handle.

As the sauce reduces, add the mango slices, which take only a couple of minutes to cook. Shake the pan occasionally. The sauce will become golden in colour and as it thickens large bubbles will form on top. When it just barely coats the back of a spoon it is ready. Altogether the sauce takes about 3 to 4 minutes to cook. Place the fish on serving plates and place a small spoonful of the sauce on top of each fillet.

FISH FILLETS IN ORANGE CREAM SAUCE

Serves 4

*4 fillets of fish,
weighing approximately 125-155 g
(4-5 oz) each*

salt and pepper

1 cup (8 fl oz) orange juice

½ cup (4 fl oz) medium dry sherry

½ cup (4 fl oz) thick cream

1 orange

Trim the fish carefully, as for this dish it must be boneless. Season with salt and pepper. Place the orange juice, sherry and a little salt and pepper in a large frying pan. Bring to the boil, add the fish and reduce the heat. There should be just the slightest bubble on the edges of the pan — it should not actually boil, just simmer gently. Poach the fish, turning once until it is tender and cooked through. Transfer with a spatula to a platter, cover and keep warm while finishing the sauce.

Increase the heat, add the cream and leave to boil until it has thickened slightly. Peel the orange, removing all the white pith and cut into segments. Place these in the liquid and heat through. Place the fish on a serving plate, pouring a little orange sauce and some segments over each portion.

FISH FILLETS WITH SPRING ONION & GINGER SAUCE

Almost any type of fish fillets which are suitable for pan cooking can be used in this dish. The flavour of the sauce dominates, so a very fine and delicate fish would not be suitable. Fillets such as snapper (sea bass) and kingfish (halibut) are ideal.

Serves 4

Sauce

½ cup (4 fl oz) water

1 tablespoon soy sauce

1 tablespoon sugar

1 tablespoon white vinegar

1 clove garlic, crushed

2 teaspoons grated fresh ginger

½ cup (about half a bunch) spring onions (scallions), chopped into small pieces

2 teaspoons cornflour (cornstarch)

Fish

4 fillets of fish, weighing about 90-100 g (3-3½ oz) each

flour

salt and pepper

1 egg

vegetable oil to cook the fish

Sauce
Place the water, soy sauce, sugar, white vinegar, garlic, ginger and spring onions in a small saucepan and cook for about 4 minutes. Mix the cornflour with a little cold water to make a paste, add to the sauce and cook, stirring until it thickens. Simmer gently for another couple of minutes and then cover and keep warm. Taste for seasoning, generally the soy sauce provides salt but the brands vary considerably.

Fish
Mix the flour with salt and pepper. Beat the egg in a small bowl. Dip the fish fillets into the flour, dust away the excess, then dip into the egg to coat both sides. Heat the oil until quite hot in a frying pan large enough not to crowd the fish. Add the fish and cook, turning once until golden on the outside and cooked through. The thickness of the fish fillets will determine the time, but do not spoil them by overcooking. Thin fillets of fish, such as whiting take about 4 minutes, thick fillets of fish, such as John Dory, about 7 minutes. Remove and drain on kitchen paper. Serve with a few spoonfuls of the sauce over the top.

Note: This mixture of flour and egg makes a thin light coating on the fish. Nicer than a batter and much faster and simpler to make.

POULTRY & GAME

DEVILLED CHICKEN BREASTS

Serves 4

4 chicken breasts

45 g (1½ oz) butter

Devil Sauce

2 teaspoons dry English mustard

2 teaspoons French mustard

1 tablespoon Worcestershire sauce

1 tablespoon tomato sauce (ketchup)

1 clove garlic, crushed

salt

breadcrumbs made from stale bread

Flatten the chicken breasts just slightly, using a rolling pin or your hands, but do not spread them out greatly. Melt the butter in a frying pan, add the chicken breasts and cook gently for a couple of minutes on each side. They will still be undercooked in the centre. While they are cooking mix up the Devil Sauce.

Devil Sauce

Mix all the ingredients in a small basin. Place the chicken on a board and make a couple of diagonal slashes on the top of each breast. Spread with the Devil Sauce, coating the top just barely to the edges as it will thin down with the warmth. Press enough crumbs over the top to lightly coat the sauce.

Put the chicken on to a greased tray or dish. Bake in a moderate oven, 180°C (350°F/Gas 4) until the chicken has cooked through. It should only take about 10 minutes. The crumbs are nicest if slightly crisp. If they are still soft, place the dish under a griller (broiler) for a moment to crisp them.

CHICKEN BREASTS WITH CAMEMBERT CHEESE

The quality of the Camembert can make or mar this dish as it is the only flavouring in the centre of the chicken. Choose one which is ripe, but which has no traces of ammonia.

When preparing the dish, take the Camembert directly from the refrigerator so it will be firm and easy to handle.

Serves 4	***Apple and Green Peppercorn Sauce***
4 chicken breasts	*500 g (1 lb) cooking apples*
salt and pepper	*3 tablespoons water*
1 Camembert cheese	*2 thin strips lemon rind*
flour	*1 tablespoon sugar*
1 egg, beaten with a teaspoon of oil	*2 teaspoons green peppercorns, crushed lightly with the back of a knife*
breadcrumbs made from stale bread	
45 g (1½ oz) butter	
2 tablespoons oil	

Chicken

Place the chicken breasts on a board between some greaseproof or wax paper and flatten gently to make them an even thickness. Season with salt and pepper. Place the inside of the breast (the ragged, uneven part) towards you. Cut the Camembert cheese into thick slices. All the cheese will not be needed unless the chicken breasts are very large. Put a slice of cheese on half of each breast and fold over to enclose.

Mix the flour with salt and pepper and dip the chicken in this first, then in the egg, and finally in the crumbs. Melt the butter and oil in a frying pan and add the chicken. Cook over a medium heat for about 15 minutes so the outside will not brown too much before the centre is heated and cooked through. Turn them over as they cook and serve with the Apple and Green Peppercorn Sauce.

Sauce

Peel and core the apples and cut them into thin slices. Place in a saucepan and add the water, lemon rind and sugar. Cover and cook, stirring occasionally for about 15 minutes or until the apple has softened to a pulp. If there is too much liquid remove the lid and boil away until the pan is almost dry. Use a wooden spoon to stir the apple, and break it up. Crush the peppercorns with the back of a knife and mix through. Leave in the pan, covered to keep warm until ready to serve.

CHICKEN BREASTS WITH CHERRIES

This dish is made with canned sweet cherries, not sour cherries. However, you can use sour cherries if you prefer, sweetening the dish at the end with some redcurrant jelly.

Serves 4

4 chicken breasts

flour

salt and pepper

45 g (1½ oz) butter

⅓ cup (2½ fl oz) red wine

⅓ cup (2½ fl oz) cherry sauce

⅓ cup (2½ fl oz) orange juice

3 thin strips of lemon peel

1 tablespoon port

12 whole cherries

Dip the chicken breasts in the flour which has been seasoned with salt and pepper. Melt the butter in a frying pan and cook the chicken until it has just changed colour. It will still be quite raw inside. Place in one layer in a shallow ovenproof dish.

Mix together the red wine, cherry juice, orange juice, lemon peel and port. Wipe out the pan in which you cooked the chicken. Add the liquid to this and bring to the boil. While the liquid is heating, remove the stones from the cherries. Taste the sauce, season with a little salt and pepper and add the cherries. Pour this over the chicken breasts in the casserole. Place the dish, uncovered, in a moderate oven, 180°C (350°F/Gas 4) and cook for about 15 minutes or until the chicken is quite tender and the sauce has reduced a little. Serve each chicken breast with cherries on top and pour a little sauce over and around it.

CHICKEN BAKED IN PORT
AND MUSHROOM SAUCE

Serves 4

1 chicken weighing 1.5 kg (3 lb) or the equivalent in ready-cut chicken portions

30 g (1 oz) butter

1 tablespoon vegetable oil

1 medium-sized white onion

125 g (4 oz) small button mushrooms

1 cup (8 fl oz) port

salt and pepper

½ cup (4 fl oz) thick cream

Cut the chicken into portions and keep them small so they will cook quickly and simultaneously. If you buy portions already cut, check that the leg is divided through all the joints as sometimes these portions are very large and will take too long to cook.

Heat the butter and oil in a frying pan. Add enough chicken pieces to form a layer but do not crowd the pan. Sauté over high heat, turning them once, until just coloured on both sides, then remove the first batch and add more. While the chicken is browning, chop the onion and trim the stalks of the mushrooms level with the caps. Scatter the onion over the base of an ovenproof casserole with a tight-fitting lid. As the chicken pieces are browned, place on top of the onion. Add the mushrooms to the same pan and toss for about 30 seconds to lightly coat them with the butter and oil. Do not worry if the butter has browned a little, unless you have actually burnt it this will not affect the taste. Add the mushrooms to the casserole.

Discard all the butter and oil and add the port to the frying pan, it will boil almost immediately. Stir to dislodge any nice brown pieces from the base, and add this liquid to the casserole, seasoning with salt and pepper.

Cover the casserole tightly and cook in a moderate oven, 180°C (350°F/Gas 4) for approximately 30 minutes or until the chicken is tender, turning it once.

Remove the chicken to a warmed dish. Pour the sauce, including the mushrooms and onion, into a large saucepan so that it will reduce quickly. Add the cream and boil rapidly until it has thickened. This should only take a couple of minutes. Spoon the sauce over the chicken, reserving ½ cup which is used to mix with the accompanying side dish of pasta.

PASTA TO ACCOMPANY
CHICKEN IN PORT & MUSHROOM SAUCE

Although any type of ribbon pasta can be used, tagliatelle is particularly good for this dish. If you can buy green tagliatelle it is even nicer, not so much for the taste, but for the presentation. In some main cities there are Italian shops where you can buy home-made green tagliatelle and obviously this is the best of all.

Serves 4

250 g (8 oz) pasta

½ cup (4 fl oz) sauce from the chicken dish

30 g (1 oz) butter

salt and pepper

Bring a large pot of water to the boil, adding salt and a couple of tablespoons of oil which helps to prevent the pasta from sticking. When at a rolling boil add the pasta and continue boiling rapidly until tender. The time taken depends on the pasta, it should be slightly firm and most dried tagliatelle takes only about 12 minutes to cook. Drain the pasta and set aside until the sauce is ready. Reheat it briefly in the saucepan and then pour the reserved sauce over it. Lastly add the butter, check the seasoning and toss.

The chicken and pasta may be placed on two separate serving dishes. Alternatively, you may make a circle of the pasta around the edge of a dish and fill the centre with the chicken and sauce.

CHICKEN WITH PIMENTO & ONIONS

Serves 4

1 chicken weighing about 1.5 kg (3 lb), cut into portions

30 g (1 oz) butter

1 tablespoon vegetable oil

salt and pepper

1 large onion

125 g (4 oz) canned pimento

1 clove garlic, crushed

¼ cup (2 fl oz) chicken stock

Topping

3 tablespoons sour cream

3 teaspoons horse-radish relish

fresh parsley, finely chopped

Melt the butter in a frying pan and add the oil. Keep the heat fairly high and add the chicken portions, a few at a time, turning them until they have changed colour. As they are browned, remove to a plate. Season with salt and pepper.

While the chicken is cooking, dice the onion finely and cut the pimento into small dice or strips. When all the chicken is cooked, add the onion to the same pan and fry for a couple of minutes. Don't allow it to brown. Remove the onion with a slotted spoon and place in the base of a casserole or gratin dish big enough to fit the chicken in one layer. Scatter the pimento over the onion and then top with the chicken. Pour the stock over this and place in a moderate oven, 180°C (350°F/Gas 4) for about 35 minutes or until the chicken is tender.

Topping
Remove the casserole from the oven, mix the cream and horse-radish in a small bowl and spoon over the top of the chicken. It will heat through in the warmth of the dish, so it is unnecessary to return it to the oven. Serve directly from the casserole, and scatter a little finely chopped parsley on top.

CHICKEN WINGS IN LEMON & GREEN PEPPERCORN SAUCE

Serves 4

1 kg (2 lb) chicken wings

1 tablespoon oil

¼ cup (2 fl oz) lemon juice

1 tablespoon soy sauce

1 teaspoon freshly grated ginger

1 clove garlic, crushed

1 tablespoon brown sugar

2 teaspoons green peppercorns, crushed roughly with the back of a knife

3 tablespoons spring onions (scallions) cut into chunky pieces for garnish

Cut the wing tip from the chicken wings. Heat the oil in a frying pan and cook them over fairly high heat until they have changed colour. If necessary, do this in several batches. While they are browning, mix the lemon juice, soy sauce, ginger, garlic, brown sugar and peppercorns together in a small basin. Transfer the wings to a casserole with a lid. Pour the lemon sauce mixture into the same frying pan and bring to the boil. Pour this over the top of the chicken and cover with a lid.

Place in a moderate oven, 180°C (350°F/Gas 4) and cook for 20 minutes. Remove the lid and cook for a further 20 minutes or until the chicken wings are tender and the sauce is glazed. Be careful that the sauce does not cook away — if the pan becomes dry, add a spoonful of water and replace the lid.

Remove the chicken wings to a dish and scatter the spring onions over the top. Serve immediately.

BAKED QUAIL WITH TURNIPS & GINGER

Serves 4

8 quail

60 g (2 oz) butter

½ clove garlic, crushed

salt and pepper

Turnips with Ginger

4 baby turnips

1½ teaspoons grated fresh ginger

salt

2 teaspoons sugar

30 g (1 oz) butter

Melt the butter and add the garlic. Brush the quail with this mixture and season well with salt and pepper. Place them close together in a baking tin. You can use a cake tin or a similar container to cook the birds, but do not use one with very deep sides.

Place the quail in a preheated oven, 190°C (375°F/Gas 5) and bake for about 25 to 30 minutes. Turn them several times as they cook. When ready, cover the tin loosely with foil and keep them warm until serving time.

Turnips with Ginger

Large turnips are too strong for this dish, so if you can't buy small ones it would be better to prepare the quail with a different garnish.

Peel the turnips and cut them into 8 sections, rather as you would cut apple wedges. Place these in a saucepan and just cover with cold water. Bring to the boil, cook for 1 minute and drain. Return to the saucepan. Add ¼ cup of water, the ginger, salt and sugar. Bring to the boil, cover and cook gently for 15 to 20 minutes or until tender. Remove the lid, add the butter and cook over a fairly high heat until they are glazed and a slightly syrupy sauce has formed around them. Place the turnips on a serving dish and arrange the quail on top. Serve immediately.

POULTRY & GAME

Salad of Snow Peas with Melon and Ham
Baked Squab with Herbs
Lemon Mould with Cherries
(see p. 16)

SprinG

Bean Salad with Prawns
Leg of Lamb Maria
Ice Cream with Coffee Sauce
(see p. 14)

SprinG

MEAT

GLAZED CORNED BEEF, SAGE'S COTTAGE

Sage's Cottage is one of Victoria's oldest farmhouses and nestles at the end of a bush track among sighing pines and thick jasmine and wisteria vines. Farmyard hens, pheasants, and guinea fowl wander in the grounds, herb gardens stretch across the back, and descendants of the Shorthorn breed of cattle originally brought to the property in the 1840s graze in the paddocks.

Leased by Alastair Herbert, Sage's Cottage is run as a restaurant, opening only a few days a week and concentrating on Australian colonial cooking. In those days brined meats were served, the brine softening and tenderising the meat as well as flavouring it. This is one of Alastair Herbert's recipes for corned beef. It is cooked in a sauce made from marmalade which glazes the meat and gives it a lovely flavour.

Serves 4

500 g (1 lb) cooked corned beef, cut into 4 slices about 2.5 cm (1 in) thick

½ cup (5 oz) bitter orange marmalade

pinch dried ginger

½ cup (4 fl oz) fresh orange juice

pepper

1 tablespoon brown sugar

Arrange the corned beef in a shallow ovenproof dish. Place the marmalade, ginger, orange juice, pepper and sugar into a small saucepan and leave to cook for 3 to 4 minutes over a medium heat, giving it an occasional stir. Pour over the top of the corned beef and place in a moderate oven, 180°C (350°F/Gas 4) for approximately 20 minutes, or until the corned beef has heated through and the sauce has glazed the top.

HAM STEAKS WITH MUSHROOM, TOMATO & PORT SAUCE

Serves 6

6 ham steaks

30 g (1 oz) butter

125 g (4 oz) mushrooms

¾ cup (6 fl oz) dry white wine

½ cup (4 fl oz) port

125 g (4 oz) ripe tomatoes

1 clove garlic, crushed

pepper

2 teaspoons cornflour (cornstarch)

3 tablespoons finely grated Parmesan cheese

Place the ham steaks so that they are slightly overlapping in a shallow ovenproof casserole. Melt the butter in a frying pan. Cut the stalks of the mushrooms level with the caps and slice them roughly, then add to the butter. Cook for about 1 minute or until they have absorbed most of the butter and are soft. Add the wine and port and cook the mixture over high heat until it has reduced by about a third.

Place the tomatoes in a small bowl and pour boiling water over them. Leave to stand for 10 seconds and remove. The skin should peel away easily. Cut the tomatoes into medium-sized dice, add to the frying pan with the garlic and cook for a few minutes or until they have softened. Season with pepper. Mix the cornflour with enough water to make a paste and stir into the mixture to thicken slightly. The sauce should have a thin, coating consistency. If it tastes a little sharp, a pinch of sugar can be added. Do not add salt: the salt from the steaks will season the sauce while it is cooking. Pour the sauce over the steaks. Scatter the Parmesan cheese in a layer on top and place, uncovered, in a moderate oven, 180°C (350°F/Gas 4) for about 15 minutes or until the sauce is bubbling and the steaks are heated through. Do not overcook — the ham becomes saltier if cooked too long. Serve on a large platter with the sauce spooned over the top.

MEAT

HAMBURGERS WITH CREAMY ONIONS

A small amount of cream is added to the meat in these hamburgers, a clever trick which I learned from James Beard, the doyen of the American food scene and prolific writer of cook books. The cream makes the meat paler in colour when cooked but adds moistness. Good quality lean minced beef can sometimes become dry when cooked; the cream will counteract this.

Serves 4

Onion Sauce

45 g (1½ oz) butter

250 g (8 oz) onions, cut in half and then into thin slices

½ cup (4 fl oz) chicken stock

¼ cup (2 fl oz) thick cream

salt and pepper to taste

Hamburgers

500 g (1 lb) finely minced beef

1 teaspoon salt

black pepper

2 tablespoons thick cream

30 g (1 oz) butter or 2 tablespoons vegetable oil

4 slices of buttered toast, crusts removed

a little French mustard

Onion Sauce

It is best to prepare the sauce first, as it takes much longer to cook than the meat. Melt the butter in a saucepan and add the onions. Stir them occasionally, cooking over medium heat, until they are just slightly tinged with gold. This will improve the flavour of the sauce. Be careful however not to let them darken. Add the chicken stock and cream and place a lid on the saucepan. Cook over low heat for 10 to 15 minutes. The onions should become very soft. Remove the lid and cook rapidly until most of the liquid has gone and the onions are creamy. Season, and keep warm while cooking the hamburgers.

Hamburgers

Place the meat in a basin, adding the salt, pepper and cream and mix well with your hands. Form into four patties.

Heat the frying pan, add the butter or oil and fry the hamburgers on both sides. They will taste better if left slightly pink in the centre.

Place a slice of toast on the plate. Spread with some mustard and then spoon the onions over the toast. Finally top with a hamburger and serve immediately.

MEAT

NOISETTES OF LAMB
WITH REDCURRANT & MINT SAUCE

A noisette of lamb is a piece of the loin of lamb which has been boned and then cut thickly into sections, each one tied into a circle. These can be ordered in advance and the butcher will do all this preparation for you. The dish could also be made using thick lamb chops and the sauce can be served with small racks of lamb which have been roasted in the oven.

Serves 4	*salt and pepper*
Sauce	*pinch nutmeg*
1 orange	*1 tablespoon finely chopped mint*
⅓ cup (4 oz) redcurrant jelly	**Lamb**
2 tablespoons port	*8 noisettes of lamb*
1 tablespoon dry English mustard	*salt and pepper*
½ cup (4 fl oz) fresh orange juice	*oil*
2 tablespoons lemon juice	

Sauce

Remove some thin slivers of peel from the orange. For the purpose, you can either use a zester or take off thin strips with a vegetable peeler and then cut these into finer strips. (You will need about a tablespoon of strips altogether.) Be careful not to dig into the bitter white pith when removing the rind. Place the strips into a saucepan, cover with cold water and bring to the boil. Leave to cook for a few minutes while preparing the sauce. Put the redcurrant jelly, port, mustard, orange juice, lemon juice, salt, pepper and nutmeg in a saucepan, heat gently and cook for about 5 minutes, leaving it to bubble. Drain the peel, add to the sauce and continue cooking for a further 10 minutes. Add the mint and keep the sauce warm. You can make the sauce in advance, it will keep for several days if refrigerated.

Lamb

As the noisettes have sufficient fat on the outside to keep them moist it is best to almost dry cook them so they do not become too rich with fat. Brush a little oil over the base of a frying pan with a pastry brush, heat the pan, add the noisettes and cook over a high heat until they have browned on one side. Turn them over, season the cooked side with salt and pepper and then cook the noisettes on the other side. Season this also as you turn again and leave to cook until they are done. This depends upon the thickness of the chops, and also your own particular taste. I think they are nicest if left a little pink in the centre. Timing will be approximately 8 to 10 minutes. Remove and drain on kitchen paper. Warm the sauce again, spoon a little over the top of each noisette and serve the remainder of the sauce separately.

MEAT

LAMB CHOPS WITH MUSHROOMS & PARSLEYED TOPPING

Serves 4

8 thick lamb chops (preferably middle loin chops)

250 g (8 oz) mushrooms, sliced thinly

30 g (1 oz) butter

salt and pepper

Crumb Topping

4 tablespoons finely chopped parsley

1 large clove garlic, crushed

1½ cups (6 oz) breadcrumbs, made from stale bread

60 g (2 oz) butter

Trim the sides of the chops of some of its fat, leaving just a thin layer. Use a toothpick to hold the tail of the chop firmly in place. Heat a heavy-based frying pan and cook the chops in the dry pan until well browned on both sides. You may need to do them in several batches. Drain on kitchen paper. Discard the fat in the pan.

Add the mushrooms, butter and salt and pepper to the same pan and cook over high heat for a couple of minutes or until the mushrooms are just softened. Set aside to cool slightly while you make the crumb topping.

Crumb Topping

Mix the parsley, garlic, crumbs and salt and pepper in a small basin. Melt the butter and add, stirring in with a fork. The mixture should just hold together, press a small amount with your fingers to check and if too dry you may need to melt a little extra butter. The quantity of butter required varies according to the type of bread the crumbs were made from and how long they have been kept.

Place some mushrooms on top of each chop, pressing down well. Then press a generous coating of the crumbs over this. Place the chops on a flat tray and bake in a moderate oven, 180°C (350°F/Gas 4) for 12 to 15 minutes. If the chops are ready and the crumbs are still soft you can place the tray under a preheated griller (broiler) for a minute or two to make the coating crunchy.

MEAT

VEAL IN CURRY CREAM WITH PEARS

Serves 4

4 thin veal schnitzels

flour

salt and pepper

30 g (1 oz) butter

2 tablespoons vegetable oil

2 tablespoons roughly chopped macadamia nuts

Sauce

30 g (1 oz) butter

1 firm (but not too hard) pear

2 teaspoons curry powder

1 cup (8 fl oz) white wine

½ cup (4 fl oz) thick cream

salt to taste

Ask the butcher to flatten the veal as thinly as possible. Dip the veal in the flour which has been seasoned with salt and pepper and shake away the excess. Heat the butter and oil in a large frying pan. You may find that unless you have an enormous pan you will have to cook the veal in two batches. When the butter is very hot, add the veal and cook, turning once, until tender.

The schnitzels should only take a couple of minutes on both sides. Transfer to a heated platter and keep warm while you make the sauce. Discard the butter and oil.

Sauce

Melt the butter in the pan. While the veal is cooking, peel the pear and cut it into quarters. Remove the core and cut the pear into thin slices. Add the pear to the pan, stir to coat with the butter and cook for 30 seconds. Add the curry powder and fry for a moment to bring out the flavour. Add the wine and cream, increase the heat to very high and cook rapidly until the mixture has reduced to a thick sauce. By this time the pear should be quite tender. Taste for seasoning.

Place the veal on serving plates and spoon a little of the pear sauce over the top. Scatter with a few macadamia nuts and serve immediately.

VEAL CHOPS WITH PAPRIKA & ONION SAUCE

Serves 4

30 g (1 oz) butter

2 medium-sized onions

1 clove garlic, finely chopped

1 tablespoon paprika

¼ cup (2 fl oz) Madeira or medium sherry

½ cup (4 fl oz) sour cream

salt and pepper

4 veal chops (or use 8 chops if they are small)

flour

2 tablespoons vegetable oil

Prepare the onion mixture first as it has the longest preparation time. Melt the butter in a pan. Peel the onions, cut them in half and placing the flat cut side down, cut across into thin slices. Add to the butter and cook them, stirring occasionally until they have softened slightly. Add the garlic, cook for 30 seconds and then add the paprika. Fry the paprika for a minute, pour in the Madeira and sour cream, season with salt and pepper and bring the mixture to the boil.

While the onion is cooking, dip the chops in flour which has been seasoned with salt and pepper. Heat the oil in a frying pan and cook them, turning until they have coloured on both sides. Place the chops in a casserole with a tight-fitting lid, not necessarily in one layer. Pour the sauce over the top, cover and bake in a moderate oven, 180°C (350°F/Gas 4) for about 30 minutes or until they are quite tender.

They will be surrounded by the pink paprika sauce and this can sometimes appear oily after cooking. When you serve the chops, stir the sauce and the oiliness will not be so noticeable.

PORK CHOPS WITH MUSTARD & CHIVE SAUCE

Serves 4

4 large pork chops or 8 smaller ones

2 tablespoons flour

salt and pepper

45 g (1½ oz) butter

1 tablespoon vegetable oil

Sauce

¾ cup (6 fl oz) thick cream

1 teaspoon finely chopped spring onions (scallions) or onion

3 teaspoons French mustard

2 tablespoons finely chopped chives

1 tablespoon dry white wine

pinch salt

white pepper

Trim away the rind from the chops and if they are very fatty, remove some of this. Place the flour on a piece of greaseproof paper and add salt and pepper. Put the butter and oil on to heat; use a large frying pan which will hold the chops in one layer. Dust the chops with the flour, put them into the pan and cook over a high heat, turning once until they are golden on both sides. Turn down the heat and continue cooking for 20 to 25 minutes or until they are tender, turning them several times.

Sauce

This can be prepared in advance, left aside and reheated for a moment before using. Place the cream, spring onions, mustard, chives, wine, salt and pepper in a small saucepan. Cook over a high heat, stirring for the first minute, until the mixture has reduced and become thick enough to coat the back of a spoon very lightly. If you are not using the sauce immediately set aside, uncovered. Remove the chops from the pan and drain them on kitchen paper. Place on heated plates and spoon a little of the sauce over the top of each chop.

MEAT

DESSERTS

APRICOTS WITH STREUSEL TOPPING

Besides using apricots you can try this dish with other fruits such as cherries, ripe peaches, or ripe plums. Apples could also be used but they take longer to cook.

Serves 4	***Streusel Topping***
500 g (1 lb) ripe apricots	*2 tablespoons brown sugar*
1 tablespoon caster (powdered) sugar	*1 tablespoon flour*
1 tablespoon brandy	*45 g (1½ oz) ground almonds*
	grated rind of 1 lemon
	60 g (2 oz) unsalted butter

Cut the apricots in half and then in quarters, removing the stone. Place them in an ungreased shallow ovenproof dish in one layer. They can overlap slightly but cook more evenly if not heaped. Sprinkle with the sugar and brandy and place in a moderate oven, 180°C (350°F/Gas 4) for 6 minutes while preparing the topping.

Streusel Topping

Place the sugar and flour in a bowl with the almonds and mix. Add the lemon rind and stir through. Cut the butter into small dice and add. Using two knives cut it through, or crumble with your fingertips, until the mixture is rather mealy and crumbly.

Scatter this over the top of the apricots and cook for a further 20 to 25 minutes. Serve hot or lukewarm with thin cream.

BANANA & PASSIONFRUIT SOUFFLÉ

Serves 4

2 large or 3 small bananas

1 tablespoon lemon juice

1 tablespoon brown rum

2 passionfruit

4 egg whites

5 tablespoons caster (powdered) sugar

Mash the bananas with a fork, you should have about 1 cup (8 fl oz) of banana pulp. Mix in the lemon juice, rum and passionfruit pulp. Beat the egg whites until stiff, gradually add the caster sugar and beat again until quite stiff and like a meringue. Fold the fruit mixture into the egg whites.

This is cooked in a soufflé dish but do not place a collar of paper around it as this takes considerable time and is only necessary if you want the soufflé to sit high above the edge. If you use a soufflé dish of 5-cup (1.25 litres) capacity, it will just puff nicely above the rim.

Butter the dish well and pour the mixture gently into it. Place in a moderate oven, 180°C (350°F/Gas 4) for about 20 minutes or until it is just firm on top.

The mixture is nicest if still slightly creamy in the centre. You can sift a little icing sugar over the top before taking it to the table but this is not necessary. Serve plain or with some thin cream.

BANANAS IN ORANGE SAUCE

Serves 4

4 whole bananas

flour

45 g (1½ oz) unsalted butter

2 tablespoons brown sugar

2 tablespoons white sugar

1 orange

½ cup (4 fl oz) orange juice

2 tablespoons orange-flavoured liqueur

Peel the bananas and dust lightly with flour. Melt the butter in a frying pan and add the bananas. Scatter the sugar over them.

Using a vegetable peeler or a zester, remove the rind from the orange. Be careful not to dig into the bitter white pith. Cut the orange rind into a few long strips. Add to the pan while the bananas are frying in the butter. They will tend to stick a little so keep turning them. The sugar will caramelise and become golden, but do not let it brown too much.

When the bananas are golden on the outside, add the orange juice. The liquid will bubble and boil instantly. Cook to dissolve any of the gritty caramel sugar pieces. When the sauce has slightly thickened (it will thicken more than usual because of the flour on the outside of the bananas), add the liqueur. Serve immediately with vanilla ice cream.

ICE CREAM WITH RICH FUDGE SAUCE & MACADAMIA NUTS

This is delicious and interesting with macadamia nuts but it can also be made with walnuts or pecan nuts.

Serves 4

45 g (1½ oz) unsalted butter

2 tablespoons brown sugar

2 tablespoons sugar

1 tablespoon golden syrup (light corn syrup)

1 tablespoon cocoa

½ cup (4 fl oz) thick cream

½ teaspoon vanilla essence

60 g (2 oz) unsalted macadamia nuts

vanilla ice cream

Melt the butter in a small saucepan. Add the sugars and cook, stirring for several minutes until the sugar has dissolved and the mixture is thick and sticky. Add the golden syrup and cocoa and stir well. Add the cream and leave to simmer gently for approximately 5 minutes until it becomes a rich thick sauce. Flavour with the vanilla.

While the sauce is cooking, roughly chop the nuts and place them in a dry frying pan. Cook, shaking the pan, until they are toasted and pale golden in colour.

Place some vanilla ice cream into a serving dish and top with the sauce. Scatter the nuts thickly over the top.

Note: If using walnuts or pecan nuts, do not toast them, just chop and sprinkle on top.

MIXED FRUIT IN MAPLE SAUCE

I use three different fruits in this dish but this combination may be varied. While fresh cherries are good with orange and banana, it is possible to use drained tinned cherries when the fresh are not in season. Alternatively, you can simply make a mixture of oranges and banana.

The most important flavouring is the maple syrup. Buy pure Canadian syrup if you can: cheap or imitation maple syrup flavourings are not good substitutes and will spoil the fruit.

Serves 4

½ cup (4 fl oz) maple syrup

grated rind of 1 orange

½ cup (4 fl oz) orange juice

1 tablespoon lemon juice

2 oranges

125 (4 oz) fresh cherries

3 bananas

1 tablespoon brandy

2 tablespoons orange-flavoured liqueur

Place the maple syrup, orange rind, orange juice and lemon juice into a frying pan and heat until it comes to the boil.

Peel the oranges, cut them in half and, placing them flat side down on a board, cut into thin slices. Remove the stalks from the cherries, peel the bananas and cut into rough chunky pieces.

Place the oranges and cherries in the syrup and cook for 3 to 4 minutes until the cherries have just softened. Add the banana and cook for about 2 minutes, turning the fruit gently. Add the brandy and orange liqueur and serve with vanilla ice cream.

DESSERTS

FLAMBÉED PEACHES

This dish can be made with either yellow or white peaches. Small peaches look best — allow two per person. They can be cooked beforehand and reheated ready to flambé before being served.

Serves 4

*8 peaches
they should be just ripe,
not too hard or green*

½ cup (4 oz) sugar

¾ cup (6 fl oz) water

¼ cup (2 fl oz) + 1 tablespoon Kirsch

2 tablespoons Grand Marnier

Peel the peaches carefully so they look even on the outside. If they are ripe they will peel easily with your fingers.

Heat the sugar and water in a saucepan and add the peaches, spooning some of the syrup over them. Cover and cook gently for about 6 minutes, turning occasionally until they are starting to heat through. Add 1 tablespoon of the Kirsch and all the Grand Marnier and cook again for a few minutes. If the peaches are ripe they barely need to be cooked. The syrup will just flavour them and they will soften slightly. Set aside if you are not ready to serve them.

Heat the peaches again, and heat the Kirsch separately. Place the peaches either on individual plates or on one large platter. Pour the syrup around. At the dining table light the Kirsch and pour a little on top of the peaches. Because of the sugar in them they will burn brilliantly for some time. Do not serve cream or ice cream; it only detracts from the flavour.

PINEAPPLE & STRAWBERRY CORONET

Serves 6

1 ripe pineapple

*1 tablespoon caster (powdered) sugar
(or more depending on the sweetness
of the pineapple)*

2 tablespoons Kirsch

1 punnet (250 g/8 oz) strawberries

3 tablespoons whipped cream

*2 teaspoons icing (confectioners')
sugar*

1 teaspoon orange flower water

Cut the top and base from the pineapple and remove the outside skin. Place the pineapple on a board and cut in half lengthwise. Remove the core from both halves and then placing them flat side down, cut into thin slices. Place these in a bowl. Mix the sugar and Kirsch together and pour over the top. Chill the pineapple.

Hull the strawberries and cut in half if small, quarters if large. Mix the cream with the icing sugar and orange flower water and stir into the strawberries. There should be just enough to bind the mixture. Chill until serving time.

A large platter will set off this dessert to best advantage or you could make individual servings on small plates. Mound the strawberries in the centre of the platter. Arrange the pineapple slices, slightly overlapping, in circles around the strawberries and spoon some of the liquid over the top.

DESSERTS

BAKED RASPBERRY ALMOND PUDDING

This pudding can be made with other fresh fruits in the base, such as loganberries, blackberries, slices of ripe apricot or ripe yellow peaches. It sets, but so lightly that it almost has a creamy texture when eaten.

Serves 4

1 punnet (250 g/8 oz) fresh raspberries

1 egg

½ cup (4 oz) caster (powdered) sugar

½ teaspoon vanilla essence

few drops almond essence

1 tablespoon plain flour

30 g (1 oz) ground almonds

½ cup (4 fl oz) thick sour cream

Put the raspberries in the base of a shallow ovenproof dish, with a 5-cup (1.25 litre) capacity. As it is best served directly from the baking dish, choose one suitable for this. Glass or clear dishes look the most attractive as you can easily see the red raspberries combined with the creamy filling.

Beat the egg, sugar, vanilla and almond essence together with a whisk until thick. Mix in the flour, ground almonds and sour cream and pour as evenly as possible over the raspberries. Place in a moderate oven, 180°C (350°F/Gas 4) and cook for 20 to 25 minutes or until lightly set. Leave to settle for about 5 minutes before serving. It can be served alone or with thin cream.

STRAWBERRIES WITH RASPBERRY SAUCE

Serves 4

2 punnets (500 g/8 oz) strawberries

1 tablespoon caster (powdered) sugar

Sauce

1 punnet (250 g/8 oz) raspberries

3 tablespoons icing (confectioners') sugar

1 tablespoon orange-flavoured liqueur

½ teaspoon vanilla essence

2 tablespoons stiffly whipped cream

Hull the strawberries and place into a bowl. Sprinkle with the sugar, stir gently and place into the refrigerator while making the sauce. Push the raspberries through a sieve and discard the seeds. Add the sugar, liqueur, vanilla and cream. If the cream doesn't mix evenly, use a whisk. Pour the sauce over the strawberries and stir to coat them all. Return to the refrigerator and keep chilled until serving time. Serve with small vanilla biscuits, it needs no more cream.

DESSERTS

STRAWBERRY SYLLABUB

Serves 4

1 punnet (250 g/8 oz) strawberries

½ cup (4 oz) caster (powdered) sugar

2 tablespoons lemon juice

3 tablespoons dry white wine

1 tablespoon brandy

1 cup (8 fl oz) thick cream

Hull the strawberries. I prefer not to wash them as it makes them too wet. Reserve a quarter of them. Cut the others in half and either put them in a food processor until they are a coarse purée or mash them on a dinner plate using the back of a fork. This only takes a minute as they do nót have to be a soft pulp — in fact the syllabub is even nicer if there are little bits of strawberry through the cream.

In a small basin mix the caster sugar with the lemon juice, wine and brandy. Whip the cream until it holds stiff peaks. Mix the strawberry pulp into the sugar-lemon mixture and gradually add it to the cream, beating continuously. It should still hold a shape when finished but will have softened considerably.

Slice the reserved strawberries and place them in four small dishes or bowls. Pour the syllabub over the top and refrigerate immediately. It will have firmed slightly by the end of the dinner.

BAKED STRAWBERRIES WITH ALMONDS

Serves 4

2 tablespoons almond slivers

½ cup (4 fl oz) apricot jam

2 tablespoons brandy

2 teaspoons brown sugar

2 punnets (500 g/1 lb) strawberries

Place the almond slivers on a tray and cook in the oven until they are a pale golden colour. Watch them carefully as they colour very quickly. If you prefer you can toast them in a dry frying pan, tossing occasionally to colour them evenly.

Place the apricot jam, brandy and brown sugar in a small saucepan and warm gently. While this is heating, hull the berries. If small, they can be left whole, but if they are large cut them in half or into thick slices. Place the berries over the base of a shallow, ovenproof dish to make a layer about 3 cm (1¼ in) deep. Pour the apricot jam through a sieve over the top of the berries and stir to mix it through. Top with the slivered almonds and place in a moderate oven, 180°C (350°F/Gas 4) for about 8 minutes or until the strawberries have heated through and the sauce is bubbling.

Note: These strawberries do not need cooking, only heating. The longer they cook, the more acidic they will become. If the strawberries are very ripe and sweet you can omit the brown sugar.

DESSERTS

INDEX

Tagliatelle with Three Cheeses
Prawns with Almond Garlic Butter
Platter of Figs & Grapes, Walnuts & Chocolate
Spiked Coffee (see p. 48)

AUTUMN

Eggs in Vinaigrette Sauce with Caviar
Split Chicken with Toasted Sesame Seeds
Peaches Madame Point
(see p. 42)

SUMMER